Making Good Assessments

a practical resource guide

Prepared by a BAAF Working Party

Sylvia Barker

Sheila Byrne

Marjorie Morrison

Marcia Spence

Published by
British Agencies for Adoption & Fostering (BAAF)
Skyline House
200 Union Street
London SE1 0LX
www.baaf.org.uk
Registered charity 275689

© BAAF 1999
Reprinted 2002, 2005

British Library Cataloguing in Publication Data
A catalogue record for this book is available from
the British Library

ISBN 1 873868 74 X

Production management by Shaila Shah
Designed by Andrew Haig & Associates
Typeset by Aldgate press
Printed by The Lavenham Press

The BAAF Working Party

Sylvia Barker is the Development Officer at BAAF and previously worked as a Consultant and Trainer in BAAF's Midlands Centre. This followed extensive experience of child and family social work, child protection, child placement and family recruitment in both statutory and voluntary agencies. She produced BAAF's Practice Note on planning for permanence and has recently co-authored BAAF's publication, *Effective Panels*.

Sheila Byrne is a Consultant in Child Placement and has worked for BAAF in the South and South West for many years. Her professional background includes residential work and ten years in a voluntary adoption agency assessing, preparing and supporting adoptive families. She combines a long experience of training and consultation with a particular interest and expertise in disruption. She has written widely on many aspects of child placement practice, currently chairs an adoption panel, and is herself an adopted person.

Marjorie Morrison is a Child Placement Consultant who has been based in the BAAF Scottish Centre for many years. This followed work in a local authority where she was actively involved in assessing families for adoption. Through working on BAAF's linking services she has a wide knowledge of the issues surrounding the needs of children who currently require substitute family placement and the challenges these present to their new families. She is a member of two adoption panels, and is co-author of *Talking about Adoption*.

Marcia Spencer, Black Issues Project Manager at BAAF, joined the project with wide experience of residential social work and adoption, fostering and group work in a local authority setting. She has a national remit as a trainer and consultant with particular responsibility for race equality. Her expertise includes work on recruiting and assessing black families, including black and white partnerships, and in working with black children. Over the years she has contributed to many BAAF publications.

Acknowledgements

We would like to acknowledge and thank the following for their help and valuable advice and comments.

Sally Baffour
Mark Cozens
Lynda Gilbert
Donal Giltinan
Bernie Heavey
Marie Hindmarsh
Alan Jackson
Alison Jones

Delores Jones
Margaret Jones-Evans
Jeanne Kaniuk
Jenny McLean
Philly Morrall
Margaret Moyes
Gillian Neish
Julia Ridgway
Margaret Riley
Miriam Steele
Ann Sutton
Pat Swainton
Sally Wassell
Lindsay Wright

Thanks also to BAAF trainers and consultants for ideas and exercises.

Finally, special thanks to the contributors to the Appendices and to those individuals who allowed us to reproduce and adapt their materials.

Funded by the Department of Health

Note
Every effort has been made to seek permission from authors to extract from their material. We have not been able to do so in every case and have included their material on the assumption that the author would have willingly given permission if we had been able to reach them.

Contents

Contents continued

Contents continued

Appendices

Foreword

Currently, there is much attention given to the importance of understanding a child's ability to make relationships with new carers. While much has been written about the reasons why this can be a difficult process, depending on the child's earlier history, there has been little produced to help practitioners and carers understand how this awareness can be applied when making placements of children. It has become clear that assessment of a child's needs prior to the placement is crucial to establishing a happy and safe future in the new family. Understanding issues of attachment and loss, therefore, are fundamental to making judgements about a child's ability to form new relationships.

Making Good Assessments is a practical resource guide which is both creative and imaginative in its format. It will be invaluable to all those faced with the task of making successful placements of children, as it includes a concise summary of this complex area of work, with useful sources of reading and exercises for practitioners, carers and children.

The Department has valued the opportunity of collaborating with BAAF in producing this resource guide as this is seen as an effective means of assisting agencies in the preparation and selection of carers, as well the matching of children with them. The material will provide an opportunity for those interested in caring for children to gain a deeper insight into their needs and to have more realistic expectations about outcomes. It is hoped that this guide will enable decisions about planning for children, and the necessary work with them, to be made with greater confidence.

I would strongly recommend this material for a range of staff working with children, decision makers, fostering and adoption panel members, and any one interested in developing an understanding of this interesting and demanding subject.

Julia Ridgway Social Services Inspector, Department of Health

Introduction

The British Agencies for Adoption and Fostering (BAAF) has been concerned for many years about encouraging and developing high standards of practice in placing children for adoption, and more recently also in other forms of permanent family placement. We have long been aware of the lack of comprehensive materials for the assessment and preparation of prospective adopters and permanent new families. The National Foster Care Association (NFCA) produces nationally available material for agencies to use in the preparation of foster carers. The provision of a grant by the Department of Health (DoH) has enabled BAAF to focus in this publication on working with issues common to all families offering *permanent* care to children.

Currently, within the broad foster care service, there is a growing recognition of the demands of the skilled tasks carried out by carers. The professionalisation of such task-centred care is evidenced through the focus on areas like payment for skills, interest in the use of NVQ and SVQ qualifications, and the growing concerns of carers about employment-related issues like provision for pensions and advice on tax issues for self-employed people. At the same time within an overall political and social framework that espouses "family values", there is an ongoing concern about planning and family placement for children who do not have a secure base within their birth family. Tackling the issues around avoidance of delay and minimising the trauma of moves within the care system will only be fully effective when there is a pool of appropriately prepared and assessed families ready to offer a full sense of permanence to the wide range of children who require this.

Our aim is to help adoption agencies and local authority family finding services develop their own assessment programmes. Over many years the concept of assessment has changed. Up to and through the peak of non-related, largely baby adoptions in the late 1960s there was an emphasis on vetting or screening. The dramatic reduction in the number of babies placed for adoption and the move to a child-centred service based on meeting the needs of older children, with all the emotional effects of experiencing loss and trauma, threw prospective adopters into the role of becoming valuable resources. This has led to a growing awareness of the role and impact of social workers in carrying out assessments; an examination of concerns such as the potential for subjectivity; sensitivity to feelings of intrusion; and recognition of the reality of the power imbalance between agencies and applicants. Alongside this is the constant struggle towards finding creative ways of conveying to applicants the potential impact of the placement of children with unhappy backgrounds into their family.

Assessment now includes many elements of preparation, training and development of self-examination and awareness. At the same time, there are the concerns that enter the public domain of ensuring the protection of children, the need for consistent standards across the country, and the pursuit of the best quality service attainable. Assessment is one part of a wider process which stretches from the earliest stages of recruitment through to long-term support. It is within this context that this resource guide has been produced.

This is the last part of a project which began with the production of some initial information for social workers and applicants. Social workers who are beginning work in this area should find the pamphlet, *Assessment: Points to consider for those assessing potential adopters and foster carers*, helpful as a starting point.

Understanding the Assessment Process: Information for prospective adopters and carers is intended to be used early on in an enquiry to give families information about what to expect if they make an application.

Key Issues in Assessment: Points to address during the assessment process is intended to be shared with families once they have decided to apply, to help set an agenda for exploring three of the main areas that are central to the assessment.

These last two are written to be generally relevant to enquirers and applicants; your agency may wish to add further information about your specific process. It is important that you consider these leaflets carefully before sharing them with enquirers or applicants as they will create expectations of the service offered by your agency.

We would also ask you to read the following sections "Before you Start" and "Maximising the use of the guide" before using the main modules.

Before you Start

In approaching this task it was necessary to define our objectives and clarify the focus and purpose of this resource guide. We were guided by four main principles.

1. Assessments of families must relate to the needs of children requiring permanent placement and be the foundation for equipping them for the task.

2. Our approach must be rooted in our philosophy of what we wish to achieve for children separated from their birth parents and we must strive for consistently high standards.

3. We need a shared understanding of the criteria by which we assess families offering permanence.

4. Assessments are carried out through a variety of means: individual and family discussion, group sessions, compilation of reports, provision of learning opportunities. You should be able to use this guide flexibly and it should be relevant to different processes.

You are asked to consider the following points about these four principles before embarking on the modules as their implications are important for the most effective use of this guide.

1. The needs of children requiring permanence

It is anticipated that before embarking on the modules which follow, social workers will be well informed about the characteristics of the group of children who need placement, the nature of the plans made for them, and the impact of these factors on new families.

It is not within the scope of this publication to discuss the important area of planning for children. It is the responsibility of authorities looking after children separated from their birth parents to ensure that their planning process addresses children's long-term needs in an effective and child-centred manner. Those less familiar with the practice issues involved in planning for adoption or foster care for children may find it helpful to read BAAF Practice Note 33 *Planning for Permanence*, the local authority circular LAC(98)20, *Adoption – Achieving the Right Balance* from the DoH and publications such as *Adoption: Theory, policy and practice* (Triseliotis *et al*, 1997) and *Concurrent Planning – From permanency planning to permanency action* (Katz *et al*, 1997).

From the point of view of developing this assessment guide it is important to state that it is based on two major assumptions:

a) As only a small number of babies are now placed for adoption, the main group of children needing placement are older and have the following characteristics:

- they will have experienced early damaging experiences including inevitably separation and loss and in most cases traumatic histories of neglect, poor parenting, or emotional, physical or sexual abuse;

- they will have spent a period of time in temporary care while plans were being made. During this time, unless there were strong contra-indications, contact with birth family members will have been encouraged;

- whether or not they can articulate it, they will have begun to form a view of the world based on their experiences. Their understanding and perception of their past history is central both to the assessment of their needs and to our knowledge of the task ahead for their new families.

The modules have therefore been devised and ordered to lead applicants towards an understanding of the needs of children awaiting placement and the impact of this on their new parents. This includes emphasising the long-term effects of damaging experiences with the consequent need for sustainable support and striving to build a bridge between applicants' initial hopes and realistic expectations. The constant challenge of conveying the impact of children scarred by earlier experiences to applicants prior to placement is recognised and it is not intended that the modules should be exhaustive in covering the topics. Rather it is important that social workers undertaking assessments view them as a frame-work for establishing a base around which other resources can be developed both prior to approval and also post approval and post placement.

b) Our second assumption is that, given the complexities of the backgrounds and experiences of this group of children, not all will be able to be placed for adoption, or would wish to be adopted. Therefore, our assessment process for applicants needs to cover both those applying to adopt and also families who wish to foster a child through to adulthood including temporary foster carers who wish to offer permanence to a child already living with them. There are key themes related to the needs of children that recur within any placement. However, the implications for children and the impact on parents/carers will differ significantly depending on whether care is temporary or permanent and whether permanence is achieved through fostering or adoption.

All carers, for example, need to be aware of the significance of birth parents and of contact issues. The focus of work around these issues, however, changes considerably when the purpose of the placement moves from facilitating reunification to building security for a child within an alternative family. The BAAF practice guide, *Contact in Permanent Placement* (1999) explores this topic.

While such issues apply to any permanent placement, social workers need to be prepared to explore with applicants not only the legal differences between fostering and adoption, but also the emotional and psychological differences.

Children may understand that they are unable to return to their birth family but may have difficulty in forming attachments within a new family. Families who wish to take on a full parenting role towards a child may struggle when he/she holds

back from belonging fully in his/her new family, or feel vulnerable in their entitlement to parent the child.

Adoption in itself will not resolve these anxieties and fostering raises other questions. Providing permanence through adoption or through fostering can carry different hopes and feelings. The use of the word "parent" rather than carer in itself indicates this. Being a parent does not stop when the young person reaches 16 or 18, nor does a young person's need for family support cease at some arbitrary age.

There is growing research about how these issues for children growing up separated from their birth parents continue into adulthood. David Howe's book, *Patterns of Adoption* and *Going Home – The return of children separated from their families* (Bullock, Little and Millham, 1993) look at different aspects of this.

Social workers using this guide need to keep up to date with the ongoing research into the outcomes for older children placed for adoption and those who grow up in other forms of care separated from their birth families.

At this point, while we continue to struggle with appropriate terminology for alternative forms of permanency other than adoption, we would direct social workers to the section in the Practice Note, *Planning for Permanence,* which lists the experiences which should enable a child to develop a "sense of permanence".

2. The philosophical context

As a specialist organisation, BAAF has its own aims and beliefs which relate to our view of the importance of family life in providing care and security for children growing up. This starts with the presumption that every effort will be made to achieve security and stability for children within their birth families. Where this proves impossible, we would argue for timely planning processes and consistently high standards of service delivery in adoption and fostering practice. Each local authority will have its own philosophy in relation to looked after children which should be clearly articulated in the children's services plans. The recent SSI report on adoption services, *For Children's Sake* (1996), indicated variations between the local authorities inspected about the use of adoption. A glance through various children's services plans will indicate the priority given to planning for the long-term security of children and how the family finding services are resourced.

The key participants in putting any authority's permanency planning strategy into action are:

- Child care workers;
- Family finding workers;
- Adoption/permanency panels.

It is important that they all share a common understanding of the concepts involved and can articulate these to other professionals, the public and the media. A strongly held philosophy that understands and values the efforts of families in reparenting hurt and traumatised children will support and underpin the recruitment, assessment, preparation and support of adoptive parents and foster carers.

The approach taken in this material emphasises the need for families to develop insight into themselves, their feelings and emotions and how they express their motivation, hopes, fears and expectations. This presupposes a relationship of trust between families and workers/agencies. The structures within which we work inevitably create an imbalance of power between applicants and workers as agency representatives. This needs to be recognised so that policies and procedures can be developed which involve families in an open and effective assessment process.

Voluntary agencies have the opportunity of being more focussed and selective in the service they offer. They normally have a clear vision of their aims and objectives which can be monitored and reviewed at intervals. Some may be assessing and preparing a wide range of prospective adopters while others may have particular projects aimed at placing identified groups of children. It is assumed that social workers looking at the following modules will be considering them in the light of their established philosophy and practice.

Agency philosophy, procedures and practice develop in different ways. Sometimes this is an evolving

process as new ideas are incorporated within the existing framework. At other times a major event like a significant piece of research, an internal audit of services, or a new piece of legislation may lead to a fundamental reassessment of the aims and objectives of the service and the foundations for this. It is within this context that we are anticipating agencies will consider the use of this resource guide. The appendices include a number of articles from agency workers in different parts of the UK about the ways they reviewed and developed their family assessment and training programmes.

3. Establishing criteria

When agencies are clear about the permanent family resources they require, there is still the complex task of defining the qualities we are looking for and how we evidence them.

> *Assessment is an imprecise process because there are no firm criteria of what qualities exactly are required to parent other people's children. Even when we know what to look for, it is not always easy to recognise the presence or absence of such qualities as maturity, stability of couple relationships, warmth and capacity for close relationships. Motivation too is a difficult attribute to evaluate.* (Triseliotis et al, 1997)

Yet social workers have a task to perform, adoption/permanency panels must make recommendations and agency decisions must be made.

The first step of establishing criteria for eligibility to apply is relatively straightforward. The more complex task is to develop a shared understanding between assessing workers and panels/agency decision makers about positive indicators for successful foster carers or adoptive parents.

Preparation programmes may include some criteria that can be shared with applicants. These may cover a range of personal qualities, attitudes, parenting skills, levels of insight and self-awareness and potential for learning and adapting. The central point is that effective assessment programmes need to have clarity about what they are looking for in applicants, what evidence they are seeking, and what skills the preparation aims to enhance. A formulation of positive indicators is included in Appendix I as a starting point for identifying criteria which can be used and adapted by your agency. This needs to be reviewed in the light of ongoing research and monitoring of outcomes.

Once criteria are established, there is a question of how they are applied. A number of agencies are now using the approach of identifying with applicants the strengths they can demonstrate and have developed in different areas, where they need further preparation, training or support, and their openness to this. This is a valuable concept in both adoption and foster care assessments as it recognises that frequently you cannot say someone does or does not have a particular skill or quality but can explore the degree to which they display it. The process around fostering, in particular the review system and the opportunities to learn through experiencing different placements, lends itself well to this. For those families offering permanency, it is necessary to think about the level of skill a family should demonstrate before embarking on a placement. In some instances it might be identified at the point of approval that families require further training opportunities before being linked with a child or that certain supports are required.

For those making decisions there is a tension between wanting to ensure that such a significant life decision is right and also the reality of knowing that no placement is perfect and there is a strong element of assessing risk.

All families will have vulnerable areas, and damaged children frequently find those areas. The long-term needs of children now being placed has brought applicants' ability to use support and be open to the involvement of professionals into sharper focus. Agencies, of course, need to ensure that they have a good post-adoption support programme.

Alongside the positive indicators emerging from research there is also some evidence of risk factors that need to be considered.* It is important to consider these alongside your own agency's experience of disruptions to obtain a balanced view of risk factors and their significance for your practice. Any experience of a disrupted placement

*see the HMSO report, *Patterns and Outcomes*, and the article by David Howe 'Adoption outcome research and practical judgement' *Adoption & Fostering*, 22:2.

is distressing and, for individual workers, may have an impact on future assessments.

In interpreting criteria and both positive and negative indicators in assessments, workers need to be aware of the issues around:

- Subjectivity;

- Cultural diversity;

- The weighting of different criteria.

This resource guide is produced to assist in the task of addressing the key issues in assessing applicants offering permanent placements. It cannot provide the final balancing that must be done in each individual application in making recommendations for approval. It is assumed that this will be part of the ongoing process available to workers through supervision and consultancy throughout an assessment and by the adoption/permanency panel. The BAAF publication, *Effective Panels,* also includes useful material about this area.

4. The elements of a preparation and assessment programme

Anyone applying to care for other people's children, whether by fostering or adoption, needs both the opportunity to learn about the task and the skills required and also the space to reflect on what it will mean for themselves as individuals and as families. There is a balance to be struck between the educative, task-centred, skills-development approaches and the development of insight and self-awareness by applicants.

Groups often form part of an assessment and preparation programme. They are an effective way of conveying information and exploring a wide range of perceptions of the material presented. Some groups may enable applicants to become aware of the feelings and emotions engendered by the topics, whether or not they are able to express these within the group. There may be particularly useful exchanges of views and experiences when group participants share common issues such as childlessness, or black applicants responding to the need for families for black children.

Any assessment, however, will not rely on a group process alone. Alongside the fact that some applicants do not find it easy to contribute within a group setting, we know that applicants need to link the material to their own experiences and talk to partners and other family members. Most agencies continue to place importance on the home study part of assessments. Ultimately the application must be presented to a panel and the assessment must demonstrate how the applicants and the agency have worked together to evidence the family's strengths in offering a placement to a child and how they will continue to work together to tackle difficult areas.

It was therefore agreed at the outset that the modules in this guide should:

- Help to provide knowledge and understanding to underpin both the professional assessment and the applicants' own assessment of themselves;

- Be able to be used flexibly within group settings, individual or family discussion;

- Fit with current thinking and philosophy but allow scope for development and adaptation to incorporate new knowledge and understanding from research;

- Provide a broadly-based backdrop that could be built on for more specific applicants, such as families offering to care for children with severe disabilities or foster carers wishing to change from temporary to permanent care.

We have therefore deliberately not attempted to construct the components in this guide into a structured group programme and expect social workers to use it flexibly and add to it to meet their own objectives.

Maximising the use of this guide

While some elements of this guide may be appropriate to use with experienced temporary carers who are changing their role to a permanent one, the material is primarily aimed at new applicants and in establishing a foundation for on-going work. It is clearly important to judge the

pacing of any material with new applicants. While some may be able to link in quickly with their own experiences, others may need time to assimilate new learning and insights. Our intention is to provide a sound base for work prior to approval. Each agency should consider what further elements they can add post approval. For example, it may be realistic to address sensitive issues such as implications of sexual abuse for children prior to approval as any family may encounter this. However, reparenting sexually abused children can justify a further training programme in its own right.

It is important that those working with both applicants and families post-approval have access to up-to-date resources. Some of the major publications and research are referred to within the guide (and full references are available in the Bibliography), as are a range of resources for applicants themselves. It is recommended that agencies note the resources mentioned including their availability and also monitor the use of journals, books, videos and other materials and their accessibility to workers and families.

Other, wider aspects of agencies' responsibilities also impinge on the assessment process. Two are worthy of note:

- It is expected that agencies will have addressed their anti-discriminatory policy, and that this will be reflected in their recruitment and assessment processes. In particular, in this context, agencies should consider their responsiveness in providing interpreters where necessary (including for the deaf), the accessibility of venues, and the overall atmosphere of welcome and recognition of applicants from different backgrounds and cultures. Social workers who are new to recruiting and assessing families from minority ethnic groups, black and white partnerships, people with disabilities or less conventional families such as same-sex partnerships, reconstituted families or single applicants, may need additional training and support.

- It is also assumed that agencies will have overall policies for their child care services in relation to ensuring the safety of children and these will equally apply in adoption. This guide therefore does not address this in detail but presupposes that:

- All the agency checks and procedures that apply in other areas of providing care for children in need or looked after children clearly also apply in this area and adoption sections in particular need to ensure they are up to date with this.

- There is already material available about safe caring particularly in foster care that should also be covered in relation to adoption.

- Opportunities should be made available for specialist home finding staff and for workers in voluntary adoption agencies to keep in touch with developments in the child protection field. This may include, for example, the growth of knowledge about dynamics and communication systems in potentially abusing families and possible factors that might alert workers to concerns.

As was stated in the previous section, this guide is not designed as a ready-made off the shelf preparation programme but is intended to be used creatively in conjunction with your own other resources. Equally the exercises are intended to be used flexibly. They may be adapted for various groups or individuals and alternative choices are suggested in some places. Some particular points which we would make in relation to this include:

• Each module includes an introduction which is aimed primarily at the assessing social worker. It is expected that social workers will have developed a fuller understanding of the topic and are familiar with the relevant literature. Much of this may also be relevant to share with applicants. However, it is recognised that applicants vary in their modes of communication and it is the responsibility of the social worker to help locate the most helpful approaches for individual families. Some suggestions for applicants are included. A growing number of applicants are finding more information through the Internet but may need some guidance in relating this to the reality of the children their agency is placing and in judging its quality. Some of the exercises included may work

differently or need adaptation depending on whether applicants are comfortable dealing with concepts and can think creatively about future scenarios, or can make more sense of ideas if they are connected to concrete experiences in their lives.

• Each agency will either have already considered or will need to consider their policy on the place of group preparation within their assessment process.

a) Are groups

• essential and are all applicants expected to attend?

• desirable and are all applicants encouraged to attend?

• an option which may be available depending on interest/numbers available/where they might fit in with a primarily home-based assessment?

b) If group work is an important part of the process, does this happen

• as the first step, followed by a home study with enquirers waiting until the next series of groups?

• as part of a planned concurrent process with the home study element fitting in with the group programme to address the applicants' personal and family issues arising from each preparation session?

• at a point when it is feasible from a practical viewpoint recognising that participants might be at different stages of their application? The need for families may mean that agencies do not wish to delay starting a home study.

c) Are your groups normally a broad preparation for adoption/permanency, or do you run more focussed groups regularly or occasionally with more specific aims? The nature of the group may affect both how it is organised and the material included. The modules in this pack are broadly based. They are intended to be suitable for a wide range of people. Agencies therefore will need to be aware that:

- Care needs to be taken in line with anti-discriminatory policy to consider the integration of individuals from minority ethnic groups, those with a disability, gender issues and prospective single carers if they are in a minority in a group.

- Some of the exercises are of a personal nature and need sensitive consideration. This may mean in some instances that these should be used primarily with individuals or families. However, some groups may be able to share at greater depth and therefore the guidelines on confidentiality and respect for individuals that are familiar with social work settings are particularly important to articulate or repeat. Some areas may be easier to share in some groups given their composition, for example, if all participants are childless sharing experiences of infertility is likely to be easier. In other instances, additional sessions for some applicants may be valuable, for example, applicants with one birth child and secondary infertility may have particular issues.

3) Some core case material is provided which can be referred to for various exercises. This was designed to develop the awareness of applicants of the wide range of experiences of looked after children and issues of potential discrimination. They would need to be supplemented where the assessment and preparation were focussed on preparing

families to parent children with disabilities or in working with black applicants around the particular needs of black children.

4) The role of experienced adopters and foster carers is recognised as particularly valuable. It is suggested that agencies continually review the ways in which they involve experienced carers. Some may become valuable co-leaders in groups and are entitled to support and training in this role. Others may be able to contribute their experiences occasionally either by talking to groups or in being prepared to meet individual applicants on a more informal basis. They are frequently a useful introduction for new families to the existing self-help groups in the area.

5) Some applications may be for specific children either because of agency policy or because of the use of publicity on behalf of a particular child. This guide obviously cannot be geared to that, but assessing workers may wish to consider points where they may need to widen their focus to a more general exploration of the themes relevant to permanence. Equally, agencies which, throughout the process, are also weaving in material about real children waiting, either in their agency or through publications like *Be My Parent* or *Adoption UK* (now called *Adoption Today*), need to consider the emotional impact for applicants both prior to approval and in the linking process.

KEY POINTS

It is expected that this guide will be used flexibly and workers should select and supplement in relation to:

- What will be useful at different stages;

- What is appropriate for groups, individuals or a family session;

- What is most suitable for the needs of different individuals or families.

Each agency needs to compile and maintain a library of resources to use in assessment and preparation.

Agencies need to provide support and training for all workers involved in assessments and have strategies for the preparation of new workers for the task.

Attachment and Loss

Essential reading for social workers

Fahlberg V, *A Child's Journey Through Placement.*
Practical focused workbook outlining developmental issues and useful tools for building and transferring attachments.

Howe D, *Attachment Theory for Social Work Practice.*
Good overview of attachment theory and implications.

INTRODUCTION

The nature and importance of attachment are as real for professionals as for the parents and children with whom we work. Each of us carries through life the impact of those early and vital relationships that help to make us who we are. Together with our genetic history and the quality of the social environment, they shape our personality and sense of self; enable us to make sense of our world; influence our cognitive, psychological and social development; and provide us with inner working models of parents and relationships.

The attachment process is complex and, because we are human, it is full of imperfections. Applicants who are considering permanence will generally need help in making sense of what attachment is and how it affects development. It is an integral aspect of placement work and it follows therefore that social workers should themselves have a thorough knowledge of attachment theory and child development together with an awareness of the implications arising from disability, ethnicity and culture. There is now a growing and informative body of written material available and practitioners need to be familiar with the essential theoretical background to the subject. For a comprehensive and relevant outline of attachment theory, the text by Howe (1995) is recommended and further reading is referred to in the following pages.

This module attempts to give a brief overview of some crucial aspects of attachment, trauma and loss that social workers will need to consider with applicants during the assessment period. The social work task is to be well informed regarding the theoretical background and so enable applicants to understand and appreciate the impact of damaging attachments on the child's capacity to respond to nurturing experiences. The background information attempts to help social workers reflect succinctly on this complex subject but can never be a substitute for professional reading, learning and preparation.

Some of this material may be suitable to share with some applicants but workers will need to assess each application and ensure that appropriate material is matched to individual needs. For example, some applicants will want to explore theoretical aspects more carefully but many others will value a basic framework supplemented by practical, jargon-free discussion of what this may mean for them and for children. Social workers should note that this module aims only to provide an introduction to attachment, trauma and loss. The understanding of applicants will develop over time and continue throughout the process of assessment, linking and placement. Subsequent modules, particularly those on *Identity, Contact* and *Positive Parenting* will complement and build on some of the concepts raised in this first module.

The foundation of attachment

Background information for social workers

Info Sheet 1	*Secure attachment* Think about the distinctions between primary and secondary attachment and the importance of connections with significant others
Info Sheet 2	*Characteristics/developmental outcomes of secure attachment* Consider the impact of attachment on the range of developmental tasks
Info Sheet 3	*Cycles of interaction* See Fahlberg (1994) pp 26–30 for explanation
Info Sheet 4	*Bonding*

Reading for applicants

Fahlberg V, *A Child's Journey through Placement*, Ch 1 pp 13-31.

'Building a relationship', *Adoption UK*, August 1994.

McNamara J, *Bruised before Birth*, Ch 3 pp 38–40, re: touch and bonding for children exposed to parental substance abuse.

'Bonding doesn't just happen' *Adoption UK*, November 1995.

All children share basic dependency needs and look to their primary carer(s) to provide them with a sense of safety, trust and consistency that facilitate learning, reciprocity, confidence and autonomy. The attachment experiences of many children needing permanence may have been highly dysfunctional and have an immense impact on their capacity to be parented by adopters/foster carers. It is therefore crucial that social workers help applicants to think about the range of attachment patterns in order to recognise the implications for adoption and fostering. It is particularly important to stress how much attachment can impact not just on the capacity to build relationships but on all aspects of development e.g. learning, thinking, tolerating stress, etc. Care should be taken to ensure that attachment is seen as a continuum and to note that within the general population a wide range of patterns exists.

How attachment develops will vary according to cultural norms. Eurocentric perceptions of attachment can exclude other relevant models which can enhance our understanding of the varied ways in which children's needs are met. For example, in some cultures great importance is attached to eye contact and visual rapport between adult and infant; in others the emphasis is more on physical closeness and availability (see Rashid, 1996). In Western cultures, primary attachment figures tend to be the child's parent(s) while in other communities with large and close kinship networks, attachments may be more diversified. Similarly it is important not to be exclusively focused on primary attachment figures, important though they are, and to recognise the immense contribution and mediating value of secondary attachments and significant others. It is necessary to be open to differing perspectives while being clear about children's emotional and developmental needs.

Bonding, or the feeling and capacity of the adult to nurture, can be affected by adult issues such as earlier unmet needs which may affect the ability to parent responsively, unrealistic expectations of both oneself and/or the child, and the emotional impact of post-placement stress. In addition, there may be a multitude of factors associated with the child such as their early experience, the circumstances of the move, temperament, disability, etc.

Attachment theory is complex and can seem overwhelming so it is important to give applicants information that is clear, relevant and succinct. This module focuses initially on understanding secure attachment and then moves on to consider avoidant and resistant patterns which are developed further in Module 6, *Positive Parenting*. The background information that forms part of this section may be helpful to social workers in illustrating the theoretical material. Some may be of use with applicants but others (e.g. synopsis of attachment types) will clearly require much explanation and discussion and, if used, may need to be built up throughout the assessment process. The exercises give some pointers for practical application and should be used with care. Attachment profoundly touches each of us and a shared exploration of personal histories, while essential, should not be approached lightly or without due consideration for emotional safety, confidentiality, and appropriate privacy.

a

INFANT ATTACHMENT

In small groups and using the attachment cycles (see Info Sheet 3), ask applicants to discuss/write down thoughts about:
• what, specifically, a baby does in order to build a relationship with an adult;
• what an adult does to build a relationship with a baby;
• if the adult does not/cannot play their part, what impact might this have for the infant?

Use the exercise to aid reflection and learning about infancy and the importance of eye contact, touch, sensory development, arousal, relaxation, stranger anxiety, etc.

b

BONDING

• Have you ever experienced difficulties in bonding with your own/someone else's child?
• Can you share something about that experience?
• What were the issues?
• How did you deal with them?

c

STAGES OF CHILD DEVELOPMENT

Encourage applicants to think more about the stages of child development. Invite them to write down alongside the developmental stages listed, the age they would normally associate with each one. Once completed, applicants could share their answers with a partner/neighbour before a broader discussion, perhaps including excerpts from a developmental chart (e.g.Fahlberg (1994), pp 80–90). Use the exercise to talk about the importance of understanding the crucial early stages of learning and development and what happens when children miss out.

Asks How? Why? What? continuously

First meaningful words

Love of silly riddles/giggly jokes

Ability to hop

First signs of peer group play

Apparently lazy and indifferent

First steps

Puberty

Fear of the dark

Temper tantrums

Smiling

Desire for privacy

Begins to respond to own name

Draws a recognisable person

Singling out a special friend

Reasonable conscience development

First signs of inner control

Begins to negotiate a way out of trouble

Secure attachment

Definition

An affectionate bond between two individuals that endures through space and time and serves to join them emotionally.

(Klaus and Kennell, 1976)

An attempt to maintain physical proximity with another person, who is usually seen as stronger. (Bretherton, 1985)

A psychological bond to a person who provides protection.

(Katz, 1994)

Purpose

Attachment behaviours promote the child's sense of security and enable him/her to develop physically, emotionally, cognitively and socially.

Formation

Attachment is formed through a consistent caring relationship between adult and child, activated as a result of stress (physical needs, threats, interrupted relationships, etc) enacted through physical care involving physical closeness and body contact which meets the child's basic needs for physical and emotional comfort. Hallmarks are reciprocity and continuity (arousal relaxation cycle/positive interaction cycle).

Characteristics/developmental outcomes of secure attachment

Sense of physical/, psychological safety protection

Trust, hope, stability

Warmth, positive attention/interaction

Positive self-image, identity, initiative, motivation

Connectedness, emotional responsiveness, sensitivity

Positive affect, self-awareness, social competence, empathy

Logical thinking, perception, learning, motor skills

Stimulation,communication, encouragement

Consequences, appropriate expectations, responsibility

Reciprocity/consistency/ predictability

Security, confidence, autonomy, resilience

Containment, capacity to cope with stress and frustration

Note: These outcomes are interwoven and ongoing. This may be helpful as a means of stimulating discussion around the ways in which attachment impacts upon a wide range of developmental tasks but needs to be explained and supplemented by a good theoretical framework.

Cycles of Interaction

The arousal-relaxation cycle

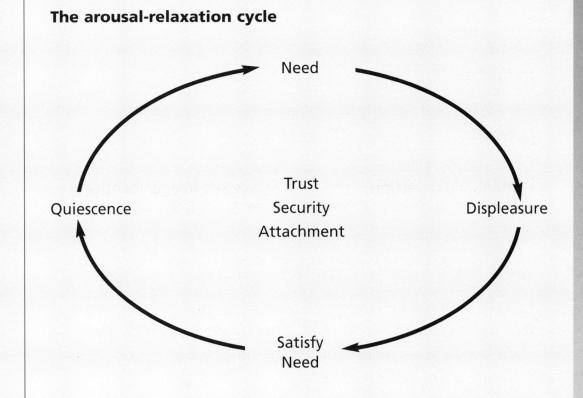

Need

Displeasure

Trust
Security
Attachment

Quiescence

Satisfy
Need

The positive interaction cycle

Parent initiates positive
interactions with the child

Self-worth
Self-esteem

Child responds
positively

Extracted from Fahlberg,1994

Bonding

Definition

The feeling and capacity of the parent to nurture and be responsive

Process – vital stages (Note: different cultural patterns of attachment and bonding behaviour; see Module 1.1 Para 2)

Prenatal – expectations, hopes, images

Birth – touch, vision, proximity, exploration, claiming, uniqueness

First six months – food, warmth, protection, focus on senses, e.g. face-to-face contact, eye contact, physical care/closeness, touch, vocal stimulation and response, specific preference

Characteristics

Warmth, availability (physical and emotional), interest, sensitivity, awareness, consistency of response, reciprocity.

Interactional nature important (temperament of child, experience of adult) quality is crucial

Note: This summary may be helpful as a means of focusing on the bonding process and what is required of the adult. It could be used to think about what circumstances/issues might encourage or inhibit bonding: what might be the effects on the infant (and adult) if bonding does not occur?

Understanding attachment, loss and trauma

Background information for social workers

Info Sheet 5 — *Implications for black children*

Info Sheet 6 — *Key features of attachment types – Synopsis*
The simpler table developed by Howe (1995) to illustrate patterns of attachment in adoption arising from his research may also be of interest.

Info Sheet 7 — *When things go wrong in attachment*
Consider this alongside previous cycles and with *Symptoms of attachment problems* (see below) e.g how children can get stuck at different stages and what the implications are for their development.

Info Sheet 8 — *Symptoms of attachment problems*
The range of problems needs to be seen as a continuum; consider the relevance of age and developmental stage; are certain parenting styles linked with certain problem areas?

Reading for applicants

- Fahlberg V, A *Child's Journey through Placement,* Ch 3, Separation and Loss

- Howe D, 'Adoption and attachment', *Adoption & Fostering,* 19 : 4, 1995

- Jewett C, *Helping Children with Separation and Loss,* Ch 3, Understanding and supporting grief

- Verrier N, *The Primal Wound*

Separation and loss

When children are separated from their family of origin, feelings of loss, confusion and guilt only serve to compound their attachment dilemmas. The age and developmental stage at which separation takes place are crucial and those that occur in the early formative years are especially traumatic. Separation frequently involves not only the loss of primary attachment figures but other significant relationships such as siblings, extended family, peers. For disabled children, physical/ mental/sensory loss can tangibly increase the sense of isolation and aloneness associated with separation. Often familiar roles and places disappear and for refugee children, and those from black and minority ethnic groups, so too may their country of birth, community, language, customs and religious practice.

A placement with a family which reflects the "race", religion and culture of the child is as important in short-term care as in long-term, and both social workers and new families need to be aware of the additional needs of black children moving from transracial placements into black families. Applicants for permanence need the opportunity to reflect on the impact upon children of separation and loss but also on their own experience whether through bereavement, migration, displacement, disability, infertility. They need to consider the subsequent vulnerabilities and strengths resulting from their experience as well as the implications for a placement.

Trauma

An increasing number of children will be needing permanent placements following highly traumatic experiences within their birth families, and sometimes within the care system. We are still learning about the implications of trauma on attachment relationships but evidence suggests (Perry, 1993) that prolonged stress throughout the early and most sensitive phase can affect the development of areas of the brain. The child's capacity to deal with anxiety, fear, frustration and unpredictability may be profoundly impaired and we are still learning about how best to help families provide compensatory experiences.

Briere (1992) discusses the impact of trauma on children's attachment behaviours and highlights the propensity for lack of trust, self awareness, and exploration, a poor sense of self and a tendency to disassociate from pain because of fear that it cannot be contained. He also points out some interesting differences in the way in which males and females react to trauma. The implications for treatment and management are particularly relevant to Module 6, *Positive Parenting*.

Many children who exhibit a disorganised pattern of attachment will have experienced trauma within their early lives, perhaps associated with abusive/neglectful parenting, domestic violence, the impact of certain mental health conditions, etc. Social workers will want to use the attachment cycles to help applicants learn about the subsequent challenges for both them and the child.

Adult issues

If we acknowledge the vital role played by attachment in terms of human development, it follows that unsatisfactory early attachments may lead to a range of dysfunctional working models in later life. Some applicants may have had quite difficult early experiences of their own that may make them especially vulnerable in the face of an angry, rejecting or controlling child.

Main's work on inter-generational attachment suggests that it is not so much the quality of past experience that determines future parenting outcome but the ability of the adult to reflect accurately and openly on the reality of their own early relationships (Main and Goldwyn, 1984). Poor early experience may result in a degree of emotional vulnerability but it may also bring considerable insight, resilience and determination. Alternatively, it may indicate a variety of risk factors such as denial, dismissiveness or a high level of anger around early experience. These may make the potential for healthy attachment less realistic particularly with emotionally needy children. At present there is insufficient knowledge about how these findings translate into adoption and foster care. However, it seems logical to assume that applicants' insight and their ability to construct a realistic script of their own experience – what Main calls 'a coherent narrative' – may tell us something about their capacity to help a child make sense of a fragmented history. Self awareness and an understanding of one's own attachment issues are therefore important aspects of assessment and preparation.

Assessing attachment

One of the most important, and difficult, tasks for any social worker, alongside the new family, is to make an informed assessment of the attachment history of the child they are considering. This can be far from easy when records are often incomplete, the child may have experienced several changes of carer and/or social worker and sometimes the only real evidence available is within their current placement. Children's narratives can help to assess the quality of their attachment systems (see Steele *et al*, 1999) as well as careful observation of reunion behaviours. It is dangerous for both workers and families to place too much emphasis on perceived progress in short-term care. Expectations and emotional agendas are very different when permanence and commitment become a reality and initial assessments may well change after placement as the individual needs and responses of a specific child become more apparent (see Module 6, *Positive Parenting*).

Understanding an attachment history requires the child's life experience to be seen in its entirety. Helping applicants to reflect on the importance of internal models of parent figures, early parenting, response to separation, patterns of behaviour, protective factors, etc, will empower them to feel confident to ask questions and, together with the social worker, seek the information they need in order to make informed decisions. It is tempting to focus on positives but the impact of early deprivation, abuse and neglect cannot be ignored. For example, a child may be seen as functioning well in terms of overt confidence and friendliness, while exhibiting behaviours which are, in fact, more indicative of diffuse attachment. Social workers need to work alongside prospective parents/carers in gathering together a child's history and experience, identifying the gaps, and understanding their emotional needs as well as the possible consequences for future family life.

Exercises for applicants

THE IMPACT OF LOSS

Using a case history from the appendices or from your own experience, illustrate the flow chart/life-line/map of a child in the care system or invite applicants to complete it themselves from the information available.

- How many significant changes/losses can they identify?
- What impact might such a history have on a child?
- What might this mean for adopters/foster carers?

This could be an effective group exercise to help applicants gain an understanding of the multiple losses and changes experienced by many children: parents, siblings, extended family, ethnic community, familiar food and customs, changes of care setting, carers, school, etc. It could lead to further discussion about the additional issues for black children if their attachments have not enabled them to tackle fundamental issues of personal development associated with "race" and culture. What then might be the implications for adopters/foster carers?

SEPARATION EXERCISE

Sculpt – Someone taking you away scenario (e.g Fahlberg, 1994, p 132) /a child being removed from a neglectful/abusive situation, etc. Discuss feelings/impact/what might make things more manageable for those concerned, especially the child.

This is another useful, though potentially painful, group exercise. Think about important issues like appropriate timing and debriefing.

PERSONAL HISTORY

Think about/draw a picture/complete a flow chart/life-line of your own life experience (blank flow chart at end of module).

- What are the happiest/most difficult memories?
- What is your experience of separation and loss?
- How were you prepared?
- Who or what helped you to get through?
- What does this exercise help you to understand about the experience of a child separated from their birth family, a child with a confused/traumatic past, a child engaged in life story work?

This exercise could be used either with individuals, partnerships or groups. However, it needs care and, depending on the situation, participants may need to be given a range of examples from which to draw e.g. changing schools, moving house as well as the more obvious emotional stresses. They should also be told beforehand exactly what feedback will be required and within groups it is usually best to invite comments on the exercise but not to place undue expectations on people. Personal responses can always be followed up in a more private setting.

The exercise could also be used to lead to discussion about the confusions of many children in the care system and the importance of good life story work which, at its best, can help them begin to make sense of what is often a troubled and muddled past.

d **ATTACHMENT EXPERIENCE**

Use the worksheet below to aid discussion about attachment memories. Remember the quality of the account is as important as the content e.g. some adults will recall mixed experiences but will have integrated these into a fluid account. The questions touch on key elements of parenting which require a capacity to be in touch with the impact of separation, loss, hurt, etc.

1. Use seven adjectives to describe each of the people who parented you as a child. This may be mother, father, grandparent or other relatives.

2. Think of a memory from childhood which involved a loss of some kind. Take time to remember how old you were, and as many other details about the situation you were in as you can remember. Then consider the following questions:

- What FEELINGS do you remember from that time?

- How did you behave? e.g. was this the way you usually behaved or did you do something unusual?

- Do you remember any physical reactions? e.g. problems in sleeping, eating, aches and pains.

- Who/what was helpful to you at the time and/or what were you wishing for?

- What might be the same/different about the way that you feel about losses or changes now?

- Who helps you when you have experiences of loss as an adult? What do they do for you, or offer to do, which you find helpful?

3. Think of a time when you were growing up when you felt really good/happy in your family.

- Describe your memory including what you now feel made this a good time.

- What part did any important adults play in this memory?

4. Think of a difficult/unhappy time in your family when you were growing up.

- What was happening?

- How were you feeling?

- Who noticed/or who would you have wanted to notice how you were feeling?

- Did anyone look after you? If so, who was this and what did they do/how did they behave which made a difference to you?

- If not, what were you wanting someone to say/do which might have made you feel better?

Taken from training material prepared by S. Wassell

e

ATTACHMENT HISTORY

Suggest applicants think about their closest attachments a) when they were a child and b) now they are adult.

- What qualities do they think of when they come to mind?
- Why do they think their parents behaved as they did while they were growing up?
- Do they think their childhood has had an influence on who they are today?

Suggest they try drawing or selecting symbols to represent important attachment figures – these symbols might be shapes, animals, objects or anything else that is meaningful to them. Then try and explain what they have drawn/chosen and why.

- What sense do they make of any difficulties?
- What was good and what do they wish had been different?

Children can participate in the symbolism part of this exercise – maybe using play materials - and often find it easier than adults! They can give very perceptive cameos of the various relationships in their life and discuss if/how they are qualitatively different.

This can be used as a way of sharing information about important others and their qualities. It can be adapted to use with existing family groups, perhaps with the help of circular questions, and can be a means of initiating discussion about how we see – and are seen by – others.

Attachment implications for black children

This information sheet asks additional key questions regarding the needs of a black child. It could be used in conjunction with Exercise 2a to help applicants think about how "race" and culture are integral aspects of attachment and how, if they are not acknowledged, children's development can be affected.

1. *Safety, protection, trust*
   - Are my primary attachments racially and culturally appropriate?
   - Will they positively help me in feeling safe and trusting within a predominantly white society where I will experience racism?

2. *Socialisation, connectedness, empathy*
   - What are the connections that make life meaningful for me?
   - Do they help me to feel a part of my racial, cultural, religious community?
   - Where can I receive genuine empathy regarding my needs and respond to this?

3. *Sense of self, identity, self-image*
   - Do my attachments help me to make sense of who I am, to understand my history, to build my self-esteem?
   - Is my ethnicity seen as an integral part of me and valued as such?
   - How am I seen by those around me?
   - Is my self-image accurate/positive?

4. *Stimulation, perception, learning*
   - Who or what are my most important images and how might they affect my perception of myself and others?
   - What racial, cultural, spiritual life skills, norms, rules, traditions am I internalising to help make sense of my world?

5. *Role definition, responsibility, reciprocity*
   - Who are my role models?
   - Can I genuinely identify with them?
   - Do they enable me to grow in terms of my own roles and to develop responsible and reciprocal relationships with black and white others?

6. *Confidence, capacity to cope with stress, frustration*
   - As a black child what particular stresses/frustrations will I have to deal with?
   - Do my attachments equip me and actively support me in confronting and managing my ability to deal with racism?

Key features of attachment types – synopsis

SECURE ATTACHMENT

Young child shows distress at separation; greets parents positively on reunion.

High level of eye contact, mutuality, clear preference for parent or carer.

Parent is consistently and appropriately responsive, alert, sensitive.

Reciprocity characterises interaction between parent and child.

Child sees parent as source of safety and security.

Child has:
- ability to form and sustain close, stable and intimate relationships
- self-confidence, self-esteem, competence, trust and empathy

Working model – MOVING TOWARDS – wanting to engage

INSECURE ATTACHMENT

- ANXIOUS/RESISTANT/AMBIVALENT

Young child is fearful, agitated when parent leaves; difficult to calm on reunion.

(Fear/anxiety can also manifest itself in an ANXIOUS/COMPLIANT pattern characterised by high dependency/compliant/eager to please behaviours which, given time, security and patient management, may decline. If highly resistant, therapeutic intervention could be needed and longer term pressures reflected by low initiative and lack of motivation can be considerable.)

Child demands parental attention yet angrily resists at same time. Ambivalence is key characteristic – need/anger, dependence/resistance.

Parent/carer is insensitive, inconsistent, unpredictable though not hostile/rejecting.
Child sees parent as not available or responsive:

- closeness and responsiveness do not last, relationships are inconsistent, unreliable;
- dependency, anger, resistance and aggression, sometimes passive;
- conflict/ambivalence characterise relationships.

Working model – MOVING AGAINST – conflictual stance
- ANXIOUS/AVOIDANT/DISMISSIVE

Young child appears unperturbed when parent leaves; ignores or avoids on return.
Watchful and wary; little discrimination, no particular preference.

Parent/carer is insensitive, indifferent to, or rejecting of signals/needs.
Parent/child interaction lacks warmth, love, attention.
Child sees parent as likely to rebuff – emotional self-sufficiency.
Child has:

- difficulty in forming and sustaining close relationships;
- avoids emotional closeness, shows fear of involvement, expectation of rejection;
- compulsive self-reliance common, low empathy, self worth.

Working Model – MOVING AWAY – self sufficient, distant

Note: Remember, many insecure patterns are reflected within the general population

- DISORGANISED

Disorganised pattern can exist alongside other patterns of attachment.
Young child's behaviour is confused, disorganised; may show elements of both avoidant and resistant behaviour.
No defensive strategy to deal with anxiety.

Parent/carer is ineffective, helpless, hostile or scary; seen as frightening or frightened (e.g. parent is abusive, involved in domestic violence, mentally ill, preoccupied with own trauma).

- anxiety/confusion unmanageable – hyper vigilance, freezing emotionally, physically or both;
- relationships are source of confusion – defensive strategy, emotional neutrality;
- neither distant nor involved; present but emotionally unaccessible.

Working model – STANDING STILL

Note: This synopsis covers a vast area of knowledge and is therefore inevitably incomplete. Professionals will clearly need to apply their own learning and reading on the subject and use material that both they and individual applicants will find most useful.

When things go wrong ...

Disturbed attachment cycle

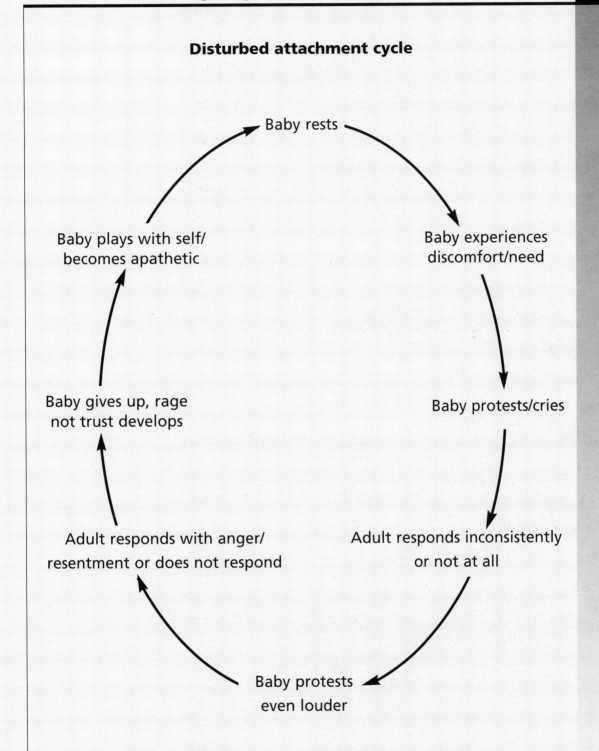

Baby rests

Baby experiences
discomfort/need

Baby plays with self/
becomes apathetic

Baby protests/cries

Baby gives up, rage
not trust develops

Adult responds inconsistently
or not at all

Adult responds with anger/
resentment or does not respond

Baby protests
even louder

Extracted from Randolph, 1994

Symptoms that are commonly seen in children with attachment problems

PSYCHOLOGICAL OR BEHAVIOURAL PROBLEMS

Conscience development

1. May not show normal anxiety following aggressive or cruel behaviour
2. May not show guilt on breaking laws or rules
3. May project blame on others

Impulse control

1. Exhibits poor control; depends upon others to provide
2. Exhibits lack of foresight
3. Has a poor attention span

Self-esteem

1. Is unable to get satisfaction from tasks well done
2. Sees self as undeserving
3. Sees self as incapable of change
4. Has difficulty having fun

Interpersonal interactions

1. Lacks trust in others
2. Demands affection but lacks depth in relationships
3. Exhibits hostile dependency
4. Needs to be in control of all situations
5. Has impaired social maturity

Emotions

1. Has trouble recognising own feelings
2. Has difficulty expressing feelings appropriately, especially anger, sadness and frustration
3. Has difficulty recognising feelings in others

Cognitive problems

1. Has trouble with basic cause and effect
2. Experiences problems with logical thinking
3. Appears to have confused thought processes
4. Has difficulty thinking ahead
5. May have an impaired sense of time
6. Has difficulties with abstract thinking

Developmental problems

1. May have difficulty with auditory processing
2. May have difficulty expressing self well verbally
3. May have gross motor problems
4. May experience delays in fine-motor adaptive skills
5. May experience delays in personal-social development
6. May have inconsistent levels of skills in all of the above areas

Extracted from Fahlberg, 1994

Building attachment

Background information for social workers

Promoting attachment
A wide repertoire of methods is necessary – these may be useful suggestions as a starter but may prove more effective for children who can respond to positive care and nurture. For others, adults will need ongoing support in order to persevere with different and alternative approaches which may change over time.

Protective Factors
See Module 5, *Impact, Survival and Growth*

Reading for applicants

Fahlberg V, *A Child's Journey through Placement*, Ch 1, pp38–45

Archer C, *Parenting the Child who Hurts* – Very good for adopters taking babies/young children

'When parents cannot bond', *Adoption UK*, November 1995.

'The milder end of attachment disorder' *Adoption UK*, November 1994.

Van Gulden H and Bartels Rabb L, *Real Parents Real Children*, Section 2 which looks at developmental, attachment and management issues for different age ranges

Monroe C, *The Child Within*

Most children needing permanent placement will have had neglectful/abusive early experiences, sometimes over a prolonged period. Although very few children in the public care system will be unattached, many will manifest a range of dysfunctional attachment behaviours described within the insecure/disorganised range. It is dangerous to underestimate the demands of caring for such children. Their inner working models and learned patterns of relating are sometimes well entrenched and the consequences for both child and parents/carers can be overwhelming. This is why information and careful reflection in the pre-placement stage is so crucial.

Many children will in time build positive healthy attachments in their new family, integrate their past and present experiences, and enter adulthood with a sense of stability and belonging. Yet the experience of adult adoptees reminds us that the interruption of primary connections has consequences which are potentially lifelong, and may result in a deep sense of personal loss and/or rejection. Warm loving parenting can diminish the pain but to pretend that it can be completely healed is not helpful, and is one of the central issues that alternative families need to consider. It is important for workers and applicants, including those involved in infant placement, to recall the basic cycles that underpin and promote attachment (see Fahlberg, 1994) and to be alert to the possibility that sometimes the bonding process may be far from straightforward. Attachment results from both stress and quiescence and learning how to calm children in order to facilitate closeness and reciprocity is crucial. Social workers need to be well versed in attachment theory in order to help and advise new parents/carers to proactively use the attachment cycles, promote security of attachment and to think about the meaning of their child's confused behaviour.

Ongoing attachment difficulties

Some children needing permanence, especially those with traumatic/abusive backgrounds, may bring with them highly dysfunctional attachment behaviours which can prove wearing for any parent figure. Careful preparation is essential in terms of helping new families to understand the child's attachment history alongside other aspects of their development and early experience. But understanding is only one part of the equation. Families (and the child/ren) may also need skilled help and ongoing support in order to persevere with and best manage difficult behaviours. Evidence suggests (Howe, 1996) that for some it is not until their children reach early adulthood that they begin to see the fruits of their commitment.

Families, and indeed social workers, cannot be expected to help our most vulnerable children, some of whom will have severe attachments disorders, without the support of a range of multi-disciplinary services. Ideally these systems need to be in place prior to placement rather than hastily put together in response to crises. While acknowledging that the availability of skilled therapeutic resources is often lacking (see Module 5, *Impact, Survival and Growth*) child psychotherapy can be a valuable tool in helping some children, particularly those who have had traumatic pre- verbal and unconscious experiences. Similarly, the contribution of a range of creative therapies, respite care, behaviour management advice, skilled consultation and/or supportive peer networks (for example, Adoption UK, formerly known as PPIAS) as well as community child and family mental health teams should not be underestimated. Module 6, *Positive Parenting*, will attempt to look more closely at behavioural issues.

Further reading for social workers

Briere J, *Child Abuse Trauma: Theory and Treatment of the Lasting Effects*

Gilligan R, 'Beyond Permanence? The importance of resilience in child placement practice and planning', *Adoption & Fostering*, 21 : 1, 1997

Jewett C, *Helping Children Cope with Separation and Loss*
Readable and practical account of how children can be helped through their grief.

Kaniuk J, 'Mental health issues for children and families: the perspectives from a placing agency' in *BAAF – AGM Seminar Papers*

Main M, 'Cross-cultural studies of attachment organisation: Recent studies, changing methodologies and the concept of conditional strategies.' *Human Development*, 33, pp48-61

Main M and Goldwyn R, 'Predicting rejection of her infant from Mother's representation of her own experience: implications for the abused-abusing inter generational cycle', *Child Abuse and Neglect*, Vol.8, pp203-17, 1984

Perry B, 'Neurodevelopment and the neurophysiology of trauma', *The APSAC Advisor,* Vol 6, 1&2 1993.
Many papers also available on the Internet

Rashid S, 'Attachment reviewed through a cultural lens' in Howe D (ed), *Attachment and Loss in Child and Family Social Work*. Collection of chapters touching on different implications of attachment in child care

Research Review, 'Forming fresh attachments in childhood: A research update', *Child and Family Social Work*, 2, pp121-127, 1997

Steele M, *et al*, 'The use of story stem narratives in assessing the inner world of the Child'

Videos

BBC, *Bringing up baby*
Shows parents with insecurely attached babies and children and how to give them the love and attention that will help them to thrive.

Channel 4, *Baby it's you*
Shows stages of development throughout childhood years, Tel: 01372 805000

a DEVELOPING ATTACHMENTS

Using the attachment cycles (see Info Sheet 3) and/or *Promoting Attachment* (Info Sheet 9) ask applicants to note what the descriptions say about the needs of one or more of the children described below and how they might approach them in terms of building attachments. Share ideas about how they might go about it.

- An eight-month-old baby girl who has moved three times and is said to be irritable, cries a lot and avoids eye contact

Needs:

Ideas:

- A five-year-old boy with a hearing disability who has just been moved from his birth family. He is having frequent tantrums which involve hitting/spitting.

Needs:

Ideas:

- A three-year-old who has been looked after by numerous relatives/friends before coming into care. She shows no reaction to changes or different carers.

Needs:

Ideas:

- A nine-year-old boy who has been sexually abused. He is fearful of males, very clingy to his foster mother and has frequent nightmares.

Needs:

Ideas:

- A seven-year-old girl – the eldest of three – from a very neglectful background who has taken responsibility for her parent and siblings. She acts like a much older child and is suspicious of adult help.

Needs:

Ideas:

- A 12-year-old boy who has had a turbulent and violent home life. He has just been excluded from school because of violence to staff and pupils.

Needs:

Ideas:

b **BUILDING RESILIENCE (APPLICANTS)**

Suggest applicants make a list of important times of their life when things have been really difficult.

- What resilience factors or strengths can they identify from these experiences that might help them to deal with stressful events? (Module 5, Info Sheet 1, *Protective Factors,* may trigger some thoughts)

- What strengths can they identify within their own children or extended family?

- What vulnerable areas have their life experiences left them with?

c **BUILDING RESILIENCE (CHILD)**

Use a case history (see Appendices) alongside *Protective Factors* (see Module 5, Info Sheet 1) to identify the protective factors for a specific child and to think about what this means for a further placement.

Promoting attachment

Responding to the arousal-relaxation cycle

Using the child's tantrums to encourage attachment

Responding to the child when he/she is physically ill

Accompanying the child to doctor and dentist

Helping the child express and cope with feelings of anger and frustration

Sharing the child's extreme excitement over his/her achievements

Helping the child cope with feelings about moving

Helping the child cope with ambivalent feelings about his/her birth family

Responding to a child who is hurt or injured

Educating the child about sexual issues

Initiating positive interactions

Making affectionate overtures: hugs, kisses, physical closeness

Reading to the child

Playing games

Going shopping together for clothes/toys for child

Going on special outings: circus, plays, or the like

Supporting the child's outside activities by providing transportation or being a group leader

Helping the child with homework when he or she needs it

Teaching the child to cook or bake

Saying 'I love you'

Teaching the child about extended family members through pictures and talk

Helping the child understand the family "jokes" or sayings

Teaching the child to participate in family activities such as bowling, camping, or skiing

Claiming behaviours

Encouraging the child to practise calling parents "mum" and "dad"

Adding a middle name to incorporate a name of family significance

Hanging pictures of child on the wall

Involving the child in family reunions and similar activities

Involving the child in grandparent visits

Including the child in family rituals

Holding religious ceremonies or other ceremonies that incorporate the child into the family

Buying new clothes for the child as a way of becoming acquainted with child's size, colour preferences, style preferences, and the like

Making statements such as 'In our family we do it this way' in supportive fashion

Sending out announcements of adoption

Extracted from Fahlberg, 1994

Flow chart

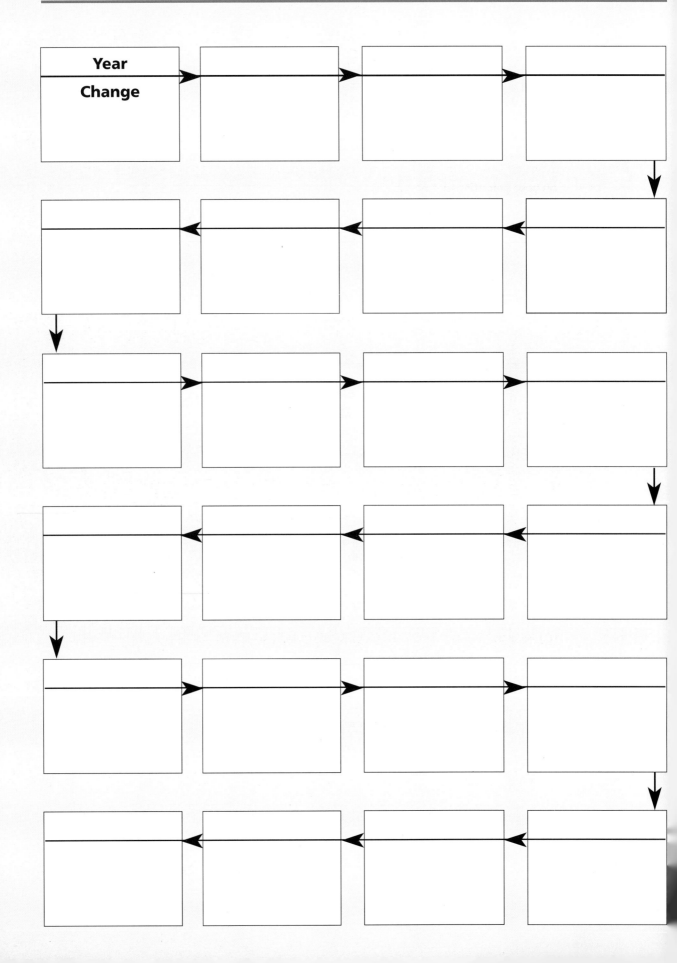

Year			
Change			

Learning points about attachment and loss

• **What new information have you learned about the importance of attachment and loss?**

....

....

• **Which of your own experiences of attachment and loss do you think are most likely to impact on your parenting and how?**

....

....

• **Which attachment patterns do you feel more/less confident in handling and why?**

....

....

• **What strengths have you identified within yourself/your family that could help a child deal with difficulties around attachment and loss?**

....

....

• **How equipped do you feel to parent a child with attachment needs? What further skills/training would you like to have?**

....

....

• **Points of agreement/difference between applicants and social worker(s)**

....

....

• **Areas for further development/training**

....

....

....

....

Identity

Essential reading for social workers

Barn R, 'Racial and Ethnic Identity' in *Working with Black Children and Adolescents in Need*

Post Adoption Centre Discussion Paper – *Explaining Adoption to children who have been adopted – How do we find the right words?*

Van Gulden H and Bartels Rabb L, *Real Parents, Real Children*, Ch 4, 'Identity and the Adopted Child'

INTRODUCTION

Identity is a complex word because it involves so many different yet interwoven layers that together make us the unique individuals that we are. Our genetic heritage and life experiences are the building blocks upon which each one of us assembles our sense of self and can shape how we fit in, or not, with our world. When children are separated from their family of origin, their genetic history is at risk of being fractured and their life experience will have been characterised by pain, loss and confusion. Identity is therefore a particularly crucial aspect of their long-term emotional and psychological development.

It will be important for applicants to think about the meaning of identity, partly in relation to themselves and their own experience, and also to consider how they might respond to the differing needs of children. This module will briefly explore some aspects of identity, trying to draw out particular issues that are relevant for adopters/foster carers and for those children needing permanent families. It relates closely with Module 5, *Impact, Survival and Growth*, as both touch on the life tasks associated with adoption, many of which are equally relevant to foster care.

The background material in this module may help social workers to discuss identity stages and needs with applicants but will obviously require explanation – see the reading list for social workers at the end of the module for suggested further reading. The exercises are possible tools which may facilitate debate and discussion but some are more sensitive than others and, where necessary, care should be taken around preparation, timing and debriefing.

Personal and social identity

Personal identity describes the way in which a person defines themselves in terms of their individuality and difference to others. This might include factors such as age, gender, "race", nationality, culture, religious affiliation, disability, sexuality, interests, talents, personality traits, family and friendship networks, etc. The ways in which individuals see themselves in relation to those around them and what makes them unique are all aspects of personal identity.

Part of our personal identity is given to us at birth such as gender, "race", nationality, genetic history; other aspects begin to be formed throughout our early vital years of development and continue throughout life as we grow, mature, make choices, forge relationships and build an evolving identity for ourselves.

'No man (or woman) is an island' and within our life experience we function within many different social situations and relate to a range of other people. In other words, we become part of a variety of groupings all of which have a part to play in determining our social identity. These might include family, ethnic community, cultural connections, nationality, friends, religious grouping, work, etc. Such social groups are an important and valued part of our daily life and how we see ourselves in relation to them will define our social identity.

Many children who have been separated from their family of origin will be confused about their personal and social identities. They may have experienced a number of moves; been cared for by different people in different places; attended a variety of play groups and schools; lost important contacts and relationships from their past; been separated not only from their family but also from their racial and religious community as well as friendship networks. The family ties which for most of us provide a secure grounding are for these children tenuous and vulnerable and a multitude of other people intrude upon their lives and their future.

Feeling or being made to feel "different" are key issues for *all* children and particularly for black/minority ethnic children and disabled children. Applicants will need to consider their own experience of difference in relation to their personal and social identities. This may enable them to identify tangible strengths they can offer to children who may feel isolated or alienated. For the child, the stigma of not living with one's family or being "in care" can weigh heavily; becoming accustomed to what it means throughout life to be adopted or fostered can take time and sensitivity; for applicants, issues such as infertility and the role adjustments demanded by adoption and foster care will also impact in different ways. Applicants will want to reflect on the development of their own identities both personally and socially in order to ensure that they feel confident in meeting the identity needs of a potentially confused and fragmented child.

Exercises for applicants

a PERSONAL IDENTITY

Name exercise – invite each person to say
something about their name e.g. why it was
chosen, how they feel about it, etc. Good
icebreaker and often leads to a useful discussion
about aspects of our identity that are important
to us.

• What does this tell us about the importance
  of children's needs and names?

b PERMANENCE AND IDENTITY

Use a case study from the Appendices and
Identity and Permanence (see Info Sheet 2).
Suggest that applicants work in small groups to
think about how this child's experience relates
to the diagram and how it may have affected
their identity.

• What needs to change and what suggestions
  can they make to enhance identity and
  promote confidence?

c INFLUENCES ON IDENTITY

Ask applicants to work on their own with a
piece of paper and to think about what impact
the following words have had on their identity:
"race" culture, class, nationality, language,
gender, sexual orientation, religion, education.

Can be a useful trigger to discussion of
attitudes towards "difference".

This could be expanded to include sharing
around what these words mean to applicants,
how important they are, what attitudes they
recall being exposed to as children regarding
"race", disability, sexual orientation, class,
religion, educational attainment, etc?

• Were these the same messages they heard
  within the wider social environment?

• If not, how did they deal with the
  inconsistencies?

• What aspects of applicants' lives and
  experience have contributed to them feeling
  good/bad regarding their self-esteem and
  identity?

The building blocks of identity and development

| Positive Outcome | – | Negative Outcome |

10–18yrs Sense of identity (vs role confusion)
Finding one's place in the world, integration

Confusion over who and what one is

6–10yrs Sense of industry (vs inferiority)
Conscience development, confidence

Unfavourable reactions cause feelings of inferiority

3–6yrs Sense of initiative (vs guilt)
Right and wrong

Fear of punishment/guilt about one's own feelings

1.5–3yrs Sense of autonomy (vs shame)
Trust in self, self-esteem

Shame and doubt about capacity for self control

0–1.5yrs Sense of trust (vs mistrust)
Trust in others, hope

Suspicion, insecurity, fear of future

Adapted from Erikson, 1963

Identity and permanence – a balancing act

PERMANENCE	IDENTITY
Security	Knowing about family of origin
Belonging	About past relationships
Family life	Fitting past with present
Being loved	Appropriate contact with important people from the past
Loving	Being valued as the person you are
	(Core racial identity)

SELF-ESTEEM

The capacity to grow and make new
and satisfying relationships as an adult

Extracted from Thoburn, 1994

Self-image and self-esteem

Info Sheet 3

Background information for social workers

Levels of children's understanding of adoption – Brodzinsky
Social workers need to have read an elaboration of this brief summary (see Further Reading) and consider how best to share relevant information with applicants.

Reading for applicants

Axline V, *Dibs in search of self*

PAC, *Thoughts on Adoption: By Black Adults Adopted by White Parents*

Wilson J, *The Story of Tracey Beaker*

Ryan T and Walker R, *Life Story Work*

Chennells P and Morrison M, *Talking about Adoption*

Self-image describes the view that we hold of ourselves in relation to others; or how we think other people see us. It is sometimes confused with self-esteem but the two can be very different. For example, a person can project a self-image that is confident and outgoing and that may indeed be how they are perceived by others. However, their self-esteem, or how they view themselves, may be far removed from that external presentation and be dominated by feelings of inadequacy or anxiety. A positive, secure and healthy identity requires a congruence to exist between self-image and self-esteem that reflects both the internal and external realities.

Children who need permanence have often experienced highly dysfunctional attachments and internalised negative or ambivalent messages from both adults and children. They may identify with role models they see as strong and powerful but that society perceives as inappropriate and unhelpful, for example, violent or abusive. They

will often carry within them feelings of guilt, responsibility, fear, powerlessness and many other emotions which will impact upon their sense of self, their achievements and their behaviour.

Good self-esteem is an important aspect of personal resilience and is influenced by secure and positive relationships together with our success in those achievements which are important to us. This can present conflicts, for example, the child whose role in parenting younger siblings may be an important part of their identity but may mean that they themselves miss out on being nurtured. How we feel about ourselves springs from our earliest experiences of warmth, safety, acceptance and attachment and the messages that we receive and absorb from significant adults. This is consolidated by a growing understanding of who we are, our own individual story, what sense we make of it and from the support and affirmation of trusted others. Consequently, we develop strengths that can enhance our sense of purpose and strategies that sustain us through the hard times.

Children separated from their families of origin are frequently confused about their past, their family circumstances and the reasons why they are placed with alternative families. Their capacity to begin to make sense of their story will vary according to their age, level of understanding, the support available to them and how their story is/has been related to them. Social workers will want to help applicants think carefully about the realities of helping children to understand their history and how to enhance their feelings of self worth.

a UNIQUENESS AND DIFFERENCE

Invite applicants to write an advertisement describing and promoting themselves in different roles e.g. friend, partner, mother/father. The exercise can be used with family members and they can also be invited to write ads for each other. It can be expanded in many different ways e.g. using circular questioning to share different perceptions – a useful trigger for exploring how people see themselves/their strengths and how others see them. Can also be used with partnerships to explore differences, strengths and vulnerabilities.

b IDENTITY AND LOSS

Ask applicants to do the exercise below. Take time and care as the exercise can be potentially painful.

- What is it that makes up people's identity?

- Now think of six words that identify you.

Write each word on a separate part of a paper doll's body. Now cut the paper doll into the six body parts. (N.B. Each paper doll needs to be on different coloured card/paper) Give one piece of your choice to the person on your right and choose one part – any part – from the person on your left.

How did it feel giving/being given? Taking/losing?

Some people give the most important/least important. Children often have no control about what is taken or given. Encourage discussion arising from the exercise about what is important about our identity, how we feel when our identity is threatened, what this means for children needing permanence, how we and they can be helped to feel whole.

Return the body parts and reassemble doll figure before moving on.

This exercise could also be adapted for using with a child's case history. Parallels can clearly be drawn with a child's experience of fragmentation and their need for healing.

c THE IMPACT OF THE PAST AND IMPLICATIONS FOR THE FUTURE

Use a case history from the Appendices.

- What messages, relating to identity, would the child have received prior to placement and what different messages would a new family need to give?

Note: Remember to consider issues arising from transracial placements where relevant as well as those arising from different family and class structures.

d COMPONENTS OF SELF WORTH

An exercise to develop thinking /discussion about self worth and the implications for permanent placement.

Part 1

Applicants are asked to think about self worth as having four major components (see below). Make a list of some things that make you feel:

- WORTHWHILE
- LOVABLE
- CAPABLE
- RESPONSIBLE

How is your behaviour affected when you feel positive about yourself?
When you feel negative?

Part 2

Applicants are asked to think about children needing permanent families:

- What self images are they most likely to bring with them?

- How could you help them to feel more positively about themselves?

- What might be the easiest/most difficult to change?

From an idea in *Foster Parent Training – A Curriculum and Resource Manual*, New York State Child Welfare Training Institute, 1985

Levels of children's understanding of adoption

Level O: aged 0–4 years

Children exhibit no understanding of adoption. This stage is not without significance or meaning, however. Children at this stage learn to categorise and learn positive and negative labels. They will learn, through non-verbal cues from those around them, whether adoption is good or bad. The task for parents during this period is to become comfortable with the use of the word "adoption" and to begin to feel relaxed about raising the issue of adoption.

Level 1: aged 4–6 years

Children fail to differentiate between birth and adoption as a way of joining families. They tend to equate birth with being adopted or believe that all children are born to one set of parents & then go to live with another set. Children need to be prepared to respond to the questioning of peers. Parents need to be able to provide them with a simple cover story e.g. Mary was too young to be a mother. She chose my Mummy and Daddy to be my parents because she knew I'd always be special to them.

Level 2: aged 6–8 years

Children clearly differentiate between adoption and birth as alternative ways of entering a family, and they accept the adoptive family relationship as permanent, but they do not understand why. They have gained an insight into biological issues. Parents need to share more concrete information with the child (more sophisticated explaining will be involved in the next stage). He needs to understand the nature of adoptive family relationships, the permanence of these, parental motives for adopting, and birth parents' motives for relinquishing. The child should be enabled to express his feelings, if it appears he is in difficulty.

Level 3: aged 8–10 years

Children differentiate between adoption and birth, but now they begin to question the permanence of the adoptive parent–child relationship. Biological parents are seen as having the potential for reclaiming the child at some unspecified time, or the adoptive family is seen as potentially undergoing some form of disruption that could lead to abandonment or relinquishment of the child. Children are developing empathy for other people at this stage, and many begin to worry about the natural parents, their adoptive parents, etc. They understand that both birth parents and adopters had felt in the past some sense of loss and this may move them. This stage of "adoptive grieving" involves the child making sense of adoption at a deeper level. Parents are asked to take the initiative during this stage in helping their child to gain a more sophisticated understanding of adoption. They need to be able to enable the child to express his feelings. The adoptive child at this stage needs sensitivity, patience, acceptance of his feelings, and support from his parents.

Level 4: aged 10–12 years

Children's description of the adoptive family relationships are characterised by a quasi-legal sense of permanence – invoking authority figures such as judges, lawyers, doctors or social workers, who in some vague way "make" the parent–child relationship permanent.

Level 5: aged 12 years+

The adoptive family relationship is now characterised as permanent, involving the legal transfer of rights and/or responsibilities for the child from the biological to the adoptive parents.

Taken from workshop material by Brodzinsky, 1990

Identity and permanence – adjustment and integration

Background information for social workers

Developmental tasks for the adopted child (See Module 5, *Impact, Survival and Growth* for tasks for adoptive parents)

Reading for applicants

Post Adoption Centre – *Explaining Adoption to Children who have been adopted – How do we find the right words?*

Extracts from NORCAP's journal

Phillips R and McWilliam E (eds), *After Adoption*, Section VIII Ch 22, 'So where are you from?' Written by a black adopted person.

Identity is never static – those early influential years are critical foundations but the wealth and variety of our ongoing experience mean that our identity is therefore open to change, development and healing throughout life. Some aspects such as our genetic background will never change but our understanding, attitudes, achievements, life choices, capacity to give and receive love can all be modified throughout our respective journeys and are often touched by major life events. For some children placement apart from their family of origin may mean a considerable loss of information about their past history, or indeed wrong or incomplete details, which threaten even more their already vulnerable sense of self.

Identity issues feature continuously throughout development but certain phases are associated with different tasks. For example, early care and attachment have a particular impact upon self-esteem; the toddler years are when young children begin to develop autonomy, mastery and individual identity; peer identity and achievement are an important part of early school years and sexual and social identity is prominent throughout puberty and adolescence. Racial identity is an ongoing process of development throughout life for *all* children although this will be experienced differently by white and black/minority ethnic children. While the young child may not understand its significance, early experience of difference and adult attitudes towards difference will impact on the black child's capacity to develop a positive, integrated sense of self. The development of racial/ethnic identity will pose particular challenges for white children (in the majority) as it will for black children (in the minority).

These distinct life tasks are faced as the years unfold for all children and parents but for those children separated from their family, all these normal developmental stages will involve additional challenges which extend beyond childhood and throughout life. For example, almost all teenagers struggle with issues around identity and independence but for the young person who is adopted or fostered this will almost

Further reading for social workers

■ Brodzinsky D, *Psychology of Adoption*

■ Maximé J, 'Some Psychological Models of Self Concept', in *Social work with Black Children and their Families*

■ Prevatt Goldstein B, *Working with Black Children with One White Parent*

■ Ryburn M, 'Adopted Children's identity and information needs', *Children & Society,* Vol 9 No 3 pp41-64

Videos

Networks – Barnardo's;

Being White; A Class Divided – Concorde Videos, 201 Felixstowe Road, Ipswich Suffolk IP3 9BJ Tel 01473 726012

certainly evoke issues from earlier years. They may be confronted by anger/sadness at what they missed when they were younger; by confusion or lack of knowledge about their past and family of origin; by the pain and fear that impending separation can arouse. Each response implies challenges for the adoptive parent/foster carer.

Recognising and making sense of these potential connections in the midst of turmoil allows the opportunity for understanding, growth and healing rather than a shared sense of rejection which can undermine family relationships. It is crucial that the long-term issues are underlined and that applicants think about the developing needs of the child/young adult through middle/late childhood, adolescence, searching and beyond. The implications for their role as adopters/foster carers, and the ongoing support services that they can access if necessary, are important to define.

a

IDENTITY DEVELOPMENT

Suggest that applicants use Erikson's stages (see Info Sheet 1) and discuss what stages of their own life, both childhood and adulthood, were the most important for them in terms of identity. Use responses to illustrate the ongoing development of identity and the long-term issues for adopted/fostered children.

- What differences do they see between the identity of an adoptive parent, a foster carer, a birth parent?

- And between an adopted child/foster child/birth child/step child?

Use the parenting circles (see Fahlberg, 1994, p149) to further this discussion.

b

EXPLAINING TO CHILDREN

Using a case study (see Appendices) ask applicants to work together on a storyline i.e. write down the words they would use to talk to a particular child about their experience. Then compare notes or provide examples from books/ stories (see Appendices).

This can be a valuable way of rehearsing difficult aspects of telling and also alert applicants to the various materials available and to agency post-placement services which could help them.

c

CHILDREN'S UNDERSTANDING OF ADOPTION

Read and discuss the Post Adoption Centre paper listed in the reading list. This helps applicants to think about the ongoing developmental needs of children and to realise that talking openly about adoption is only the first step and needs to be followed by explaining and exploring.

Discuss in relation to developmental tasks for the adopted child/adult (see Info Sheet 4), linking with earlier material around separation, loss and attachment and thinking about different needs and implications for parenting throughout the life cycle.

d

MEETING LIFETIME NEEDS

Invite an adopted person to talk or show a video of an adult adoptee speaking about their experience and feelings; read and discuss an account of a reunion from NORCAP's journal; encourage applicants to think about the critical phases in childhood/adulthood for adopted children using appropriate material (see Info Sheet 4), the longer term issues involved in permanence, and their hopes and fears.

Developmental tasks for adoptees (childhood)

PHASE	GOALS/TASKS	POSSIBLE ISSUES FOR ADOPTEES (Building on earlier phases)
Pre birth	• **Survival/development**	• Genetic heritage • Pre birth environment (eg. drugs, alcohol)
Baby/toddler	• **Surviving any birth family** separations • **Physical and emotional** development/milestones • **Experiencing** security/nurturing	• Separation, loss, grieving • Adapting to new family • Recovery from physical or emotional hurt • Limitations on verbal communication • Developing or transferring bonding/attachment
Pre school child	• **Developing/expressing** relationships and trust with adults • **Growth of** initiative/autonomy • **Ability to play** • **Learning to deal with** anger and aggression/use self-control • **Learning to relate to** other children	• Receiving early information on adoption • Developing self-esteem • Learning different patterns of relating/behaviour • Possible regression if earlier unresolved grief • Potential issues re: trust, play, self-control, peer relationships depending on early adverse experience
School age child	• **Developing family** relationships • **Appropriate** emotional/behavioural development • **Affirming permanency of** family membership • **Ability to function well in** wider social environment (eg. school/community) • **Able to form/sustain** relationships with peers	• Coping with feelings of ambivalence re: need for placement • Awareness of meaning of adoption • Knowledge and understanding of having two families • Anxiety about permanency of adoptive relationship • Contact/no contact with birth family • Dealing with family/community responses to adoption • Struggling with self-esteem and identity issues
Puberty and adolescence	• **Confronting genetic and psychological parts of self** • **Forming an integrated** identity • **Sexual development,** identity, relationships • **Achieving appropriate** and successful independence	• Dealing with sexuality/non incest taboo • Contact or tracing issues • Nature/degree of identification with adoptive and birth families • Integrating genetic and adoptive identity • Early pain/loss may be reactivated by developmental stage • Achieving independence may be affected by earlier separation experience

Developmental tasks for adoptees (adulthood)

PHASE	GOALS/TASKS	ISSUES FOR ADOPTEE
Young adult	• **Making choices regarding** adult relationships/lifestyle • **Education/career** development • **Considering forming** permanent relationship with another adult • **Reviewing/reaffirming ties** with adoptive family	• Achieving appropriate independence • Genealogical continuity • Capacity to trust/relate may be affected by earlier pain • Renewed or continuing interest in birth family • Deciding to search or not (including birth sibs/"others") and dealing with outcome • Awareness of specific genetic issues/risks eg. health • Exploring moral/spiritual implications of adoption • Managing emotional impact/implications of searching and contact • Building an integrated adult identity with incomplete/difficult information
Adulthood	• **Becoming a parent** • **Understanding own** parenting experiences • **Understanding the** importance of both biological and psychological past	• Accepting shift in generational roles • Reminder of adoption circumstances at critical life stages • Genealogical discontinuity with adopters as grandparents • Experiencing death of both adoptive and birth parents • "Retelling" adoption to own children • Establishing long-term roles for both adoptive/birth families • Acknowledging growing importance of birth siblings • Understanding the impact of both biological and psychological past

Adapted from Rosenberg, 1992

Learning points about identity

- What new thoughts have you had about identity issues generally?

....
....

- What aspects of your own identity have you been made more aware of? What strengths or vulnerable areas have you identified?

....
....

- In what way do you now feel you understand more about the identity needs of children separated from their families?

....
....

- What are your hopes and fears about the identity development of a child who may be placed with you? Having considered the long-term implications, which stages are you more/less confident about managing?

....
....

- What resources have you identified in terms of where you might go for help or advice should you need it?

....
....

- Points of agreement/difference between applicant(s) and social worker(s)

....
....

- Areas for further training/development

....
....
....
....

MODULE

3

Contact

Essential reading for social workers

Contact in Permanent Placements, BAAF

Fratter J, *Adoption with Contact – Implications for Policy and Practice*

Smith G, 'Do children have the right to leave their past behind them?' in *See You Soon*
Covers contact issues in relation to children who have been sexually abused, exploring reasons for not planning any contact.

Extracts from some of the suggested reading, either above or at the end of this module, may be helpful to share with applicants for example: the discussion of children's wishes in *Contact: Managing Visits to Children looked after away from home* (Hess & Proch,1994), page 42 and the paragraph re. changing needs over time in *See You Soon,* (Argent, 1995) page 202.

It is also of particular importance in the field of contact that workers continue to update themselves on the small but growing body of research and practice studies

INTRODUCTION

Research on contact in permanent placement, whether indirect or direct, is as yet limited but does indicate it can be successful in every type of placement, including adoption, if the adults concerned can reach agreement and work together in the best interest of the child. However, research also points out some potential pitfalls. Contact can become a bargaining tool between adults or with agencies and is then not child-centred. Adults may not be able to work together co-operatively, or the placement may be undermined when permanence outside the birth family has not been fully accepted by all involved. It is also easy to overlook important relationships other than those with birth parents, particularly siblings, extended family, previous carers and significant others, including relationships with other children. Issues of "race", disability, gender and class are often ignored, underestimated, or may be inappropriately dealt with, for example, in making placement and contact plans for sibling groups. Frequently, too short a time scale is taken in assessing the child's contact needs. Contact decisions in childhood should be based on balancing the life-time issues for the child with the more immediate circumstances, particularly the child's previous life history and existing pattern of relationships. In some instances contact (particularly direct) may not be appropriate.

Keeping contact decisions child-centred and any arrangements for contact child-focussed are extremely difficult tasks. Adults agendas can only too easily get in the way of appropriate planning and decision making and may determine how far the plans made are actually carried through after placement with an alternative family.

This module aims to develop applicants' understanding of the importance and complexity of openness and contact issues for the child, their new permanent family and the birth family. It explores the impact on applicants' own feelings, and their understanding of the implications of contact for all members of their family.

Opportunities are also provided for applicants to explore and address the child's own wishes and feelings, and those of birth families and significant others from the child's past.

Contact issues are generally very complex – however, it is important that applicants and their families are not overawed or overwhelmed for contact issues can provide some of the most powerful tools in working with children to forge sound relationships and to make good provision for their futures. The following exercises will help you alert applicants to some of the issues and enable them to consider how they might tackle these and what areas they need to work on further. Some exercises could usefully be worked on in groups, others may be more appropriate for individual/family reflection using some of the suggested reading to supplement this.

The themes within this module are also addressed in greater detail in BAAF's Good Practice Guide, *Contact in Permanent Placement*.

Permanent families and contact

Background information for social workers

Info Sheet 1	*Openness in permanent placements*
Info Sheet 2	*Examples of contact in permanent placements*
Info Sheet 3	*Indirect rather than no contact?*

Reading for applicants

Examples from Fratter J, *Adoption with Contact*

'Dilemma', a poem, *Adoption UK,* November 1996, no.79

Verity P, 'Foster carers and contact' in Argent H, *See you Soon*
Not specifically about permanent placements, but covers a wide range of issues and experiences for carers.

'One Family's Experience of Contact', *Adoption UK,* February 1994, no. 68

Although planned contact may be first and foremost for the child's welfare, it inevitably calls into play strong emotional responses in families. Contact acts as an unavoidable reminder that the child involved was born into another family, not that of the applicants. This can act as a painful reminder of infertility or sharpen any lingering feelings of resentment or anxiety families may have towards birth parents who may have neglected the child or who seem perhaps to lead a disturbing lifestyle through drug or alcohol abuse. However, contact can also help families to keep in focus the child's need to acknowledge who they are, to grieve for past losses, and to prepare in every way for an adulthood which will build on and come to terms with their past. Families should be helped to develop a balanced view of contact issues; many will also experience positive benefits from contact for themselves, as well as through the support it may give to their growing relationship with the child.

In considering how well new permanent families can meet children's needs it is important to help them begin with their own preconceptions and feelings about contact.

• How far do they acknowledge or understand these as a prerequisite to learning to deal with them effectively?

• Have the applicants had previous involvement with contact as foster carers or heard about successful or unsuccessful experiences through their family or friends?

• Do they have knowledge or preconceptions drawn from accounts in the media eg. of tracing issues or adult reunions?

Whatever the source of their information, a growing self-awareness about their own wishes and feelings as well as the capacity to acknowledge children's needs and continue to learn about contact from the experiences of others or from research is essential.

a

THE CONTINUUM OF CONTACT

Ask applicants to think about the continuum of contact and where they fall on this, both before and after a group or family discussion.

- Why are they where they are on the continuum?

- What personal, family, wider group or community experiences have formed this view?

- Who or what might change it?

b

HOW IMPORTANT IN MAKING DECISIONS IS THE 'HERE AND NOW' AND THE 'FUTURE'?

The following will help applicants think about the values they attach to long-term family knowledge and relationships, and how these change over time.

- How has your view of your own family network changed since childhood?

- Who was important to you then? And now?

- Draw a diagram with yourself in the centre using strong, weak and stressful lines of connection.

c

WHAT FEELINGS DOES THE IDEA OF CONTACT AROUSE?

Make up a set of cards from Information Sheet 2, *Examples of Contact in Permanent Placements,* listing some of the possible types of contact.
Participants should pick up the cards in turn and discuss as a small group what positives they see, or fears and anxieties they hold, for each example.

What does this tell participants about:

- Their feelings?

- The implications of these for a child?

Openness in permanent placements

- Involving birth families in choice of or discussions about the alternative family placement

- Exchange of information between birth family members and prospective adopters/foster carers prior to placement

- Adopters and birth parents meeting on a "one off" basis, irrespective of whether there is a plan for contact after placement

- The noting of updating information, from one or more parties to an adoption placement, on agency files

- Direct or indirect contact between a child and/or her or his adopters/foster carers and members of the birth family

Examples of contact in permanent placements

May be with a wide range of people including:

- birth parents
- siblings
- members of extended family network
- previous carers and their children
- child's friends
- significant others

Forms of direct contact may include:

- exchange of letters, cards, presents
- audio tapes, videos, photographs, letters or telephone calls
- face-to-face meetings (at home or at a neutral venue)

Indirect contact may include:

- communication via a third party (eg 'letterbox' via agency)
- adult-to-adult contact excluding the child

Indirect rather than no contact?

ISSUES FOR FAMILY OR GROUP DISCUSSION

Advantages for adoptive parents/foster carers

- Based on reality, not fantasy

- No secrets in the family

- A communication route to build on

- Updates knowledge about birth family

Can you add others?

-

-

Drawbacks for carers

- Reminder of birth parents pain

- Feelings of guilt about child

- May be difficult to 'protect' child fully from emotional or sexual pressures

Can you add others?

-

-

Questions to consider

- How far are the advantages/drawbacks the same/different for everyone in the permanent family – the adoptive parents/foster carers, existing children (birth, stepchildren, fostered or adopted)?

- What are the issues for the child placed?

- How can advantages be maximised/drawbacks minimised?

- What if there is no indirect contact? Identify implications now and for the future.

Children's needs

Background information for social workers

Info Sheet 4 *The role of contact in permanence*

Reading for applicants

'Denying Contact is Wrong', *Adoption UK*, February 1995, no.72

'The Impact of the Past', *Adoption UK*, Nov 1994, no. 71

'A Ghost in my Country', *Adoption & Fostering*, 21 : 2, 1996

'Dream's End', *Adoption & Fostering*, 21 : 2 1997.

Both articles are by Ji Sun Sjögren and explore issues arising from intercountry adoption but have identity implications relevant for all permanent carers

Dickson V, 'A Care Leaver's Perspective of Care and Contact' in Argent H, *See You Soon*

Knowledge and understanding of his or her family background, history and early relationships are vital for every child's identity both as a key to the past and as a resource for the future. This openness can be achieved either through the collection and exchange of information, or through direct or indirect communication between the child and family members or other significant people from the past, that is, through some form of contact.

All planning and decision making about contact must be child-centred and clearly made in the best interests of the child.

Children themselves may not find it easy to express their wishes and feelings about contact but these should always be listened to. Where children's wishes are either unrealistic or not in their best interests this situation will need to be handled with particular sensitivity. Adoptive parents and foster carers families can be helped in their role by developing an understanding that contact issues can also provide the opportunity for them to build a deeper and more trusting relationship with the child who will carry powerful psychological images of the birth family even if she/he may not consciously remember them.

The term "contact" is often used as a shorthand expression for actual meetings but it is important to remember that there is a range of possible types of contact, both indirect and direct. When contact in relation to any placement is being discussed, it is vital from the start to clarify what is being meant. This should include who it is anticipated will be involved as well as why, and when and where the contact will take place.

For some children, perhaps because of the particular pattern of past abuse, contact will not be appropriate. But it must be remembered that lack of contact does not necessarily mean a severance of connection from the birth family.

In those cases where a sound and thorough assessment has been made of the child's need for some form of contact to take place, this should enable families to have confidence in the decisions made. Nevertheless, workers will need to bear in mind that families need sufficient time to come to an understanding of the child's particular needs and situation before they can commit themselves fully to the plan proposed.

Just as every child is unique, so every contact plan will be unique to a particular child's history/experiences/developmental stage. Such plans will need to be adapted over time if they are to continue meeting a child's needs at every stage of her/his development. Children's own perspectives and needs will also change over time, particularly during adolescence, and will increasingly influence the plans for contact (or no contact) and the nature of any arrangements made.

Exercises for applicants

CHILDREN'S WISHES AND FEELINGS

What might prevent children from being open about their feelings in relation to contact:

- When they have just been placed in an alternative family?

- When they are a young adult i.e. 18 or more?

THE ADVANTAGES/DISADVANTAGES OF CONTACT

Make up a set of cards using Information Sheet 2, *Examples of Contact in Permanent Placement*. Participants pick up the cards in turn and as a group (or splitting into 3 small groups) put themselves in turn in the place of a) the child b) the birth family and c) the new permanent family. For each role, participants should consider the following:

- How could you turn a potential disadvantage of contact into an advantage?

- What might change an advantage into a disadvantage?

- How might you prevent this happening?

CONFLICTING NEEDS WITHIN THE SIBLING GROUP

Take a sibling case study from the Appendices or your your own experience and, using Information Sheet 4, *The Role of Contact in Permanence*, ask families to consider the following questions:

- What is important in relation to contact for children's present security and attachments? For future development? Do these differ and, if so, why?

- Talk about or write down what you see as each child's contact needs.
    a) Short term
    b) Long term

- What different contact needs are there within the sibling group? How could you work with these?

Social workers may also need to encourage families to look at the differing needs of children adopted at different times or where the permanent family has a combination of birth, step, fostered or adopted children.

The role of contact in permanence

- Enabling the child to develop a realistic understanding of the circumstances of separation

- Enabling a child to grieve for his or her loss

- Enabling a child to move on and develop new attachments with the blessing of her or his parents

- Maintaining a flow of communication which could facilitate future contact

- Need for direct information (re: self/family history)

- Reassurance about well-being of family members and friends

- Constructing a full sense of identity including "race", culture, religion, language

- Establishing appropriate role of the birth family (present and future)

- Enabling sense of reality to replace fantasies

- Retaining valuable relationships

- Meeting child's needs for "no contact" – either at time of placement or later

Developing contact skills

Effective contact skills require that you appreciate, understand and work with the viewpoint and wishes of all those involved – adults as well as the child and also any siblings or children already living within the new family. Some contact may be supervised or held in a neutral venue and agencies increasingly offer mediation or support services for adopters as well as for foster carers. However, some adopters and foster carers will find themselves needing to take responsibility for planning, negotiating and managing contact throughout the future years of placement and sometimes this may be without access to very much in the way of ongoing social work support. Many families could be helped by having access to parents/carers' support groups where experiences and ideas can be shared and encouragement or help offered. It is important that alternative families are given information about such groups and any available social work support at an early stage of their preparation and approval.

Agreed contact is likely to be much more effective in meeting the child's needs and adapting to his or her developmental stages than contact that has been agreed or "imposed" whether by court or agency. In all permanent placements agencies need to continue to offer support in monitoring, reviewing and renegotiating contact when requested. However, in fostering placements it is important to bear in mind that the agency also retains legal responsibility for the child throughout his or her childhood including decisions about contact (for more details see BAAF's Good Practice Guide, *Contact in Permanent Placements*).

All applicants will need to consider their abilities in relation to managing contact for children placed. They will also need to be able to play an appropriate role in reassessing and renegotiating contact arrangements throughout childhood and adolescence and be prepared to support those young people or adults who decide to trace in later years. Situations where it has been decided that it is not appropriate for the child to maintain any contact, or to discontinue existing contact during the placement, will equally require sensitivity and skills on the part of permanent families.

a

CONFLICT OF WISHES

Next week is

- the anniversary of your meeting (partnership)
- your wedding anniversary
- your mother's 80th birthday (single carer)

Your adoptive children's birth mother tells them on the telephone that she wants to see them on that date, which is also her own birthday, for the first time since placement – otherwise she will be on her own.

In pairs, one take the adoptive parent's role and the other the birth mother's and discuss.

- How did you feel?
- Whose needs were you thinking about?
- How might this situation have been prevented?

Feedback first to each other and then to the group.

b

APPRECIATING HOW OTHERS FEEL (exploring issues of concern to birth relatives)

Using a case study from the Appendices or your own experience, consider the following situation: The birth parent wants to meet the adopters.

How does each party feel about initiating contact in relation to:

- themselves
- each other
- any other children in either family

How might this situation best be taken forward?

c

DIFFICULT SITUATIONS IN CONTACT

Your five-year-old foster child's birth father arrives as arranged to see her on her birthday. He brings her a tent as her birthday present and suggests that they have a pretend teddy bears picnic inside it. Your nine-year-old daughter also wants to join in. You are supervising the visit as there has been a previous disclosure of sexual abuse by the foster child's elder sister aged 10. Your five-year-old foster child is very keen to see her father.

- What do you feel?
- What do you do?
- What might have helped prevent this particular situation?

For adopters: If a similar situation arose for you, how would you handle it?

Group work: Use the above exercise as a sculpt.

d **REASSESSING CONTACT**

Amy and Samantha are half-sisters aged six and three placed with you a year ago. There has only been letter box contact between you and their mother who has drug and alcohol problems. You know that Amy, although happy with you, worries a great deal about her mother. One day you receive a letter from Amy's mother saying she has had a further course of drug treatment and also has a new partner. He is a single father successfully bringing up two teenage sons as well as holding down a steady job. The birth mother asks if you will bring both children to see her, either in a local park or at the Social Services office if you would prefer this.

- How do you decide what might be best for the children?

- What are the implications for you of this request? (Identify your hopes and fears for the future as well as those in the present.)

- What are the practical issues involved?

- Who might help you talk it over?

e **PLANNING FOR CONTACT**

Return to the previous case study about Amy and Samantha. You have decided to meet their mother and her new partner, without the children initially, at the Social Services office.

- How would you prepare for this meeting? (Identify your thinking/feelings as well as the action you take.)

- Who is involved?

- What do you discuss and how do you keep the children's needs at the forefront?

- If the children are to meet their mother, what is to be decided?

- What if you cannot reach agreement over the best way forward?

Planning for contact/no contact

Issues for family or group discussion

Consider both direct and indirect contact and then the following:

- Being clear about the current plan for contact/no contact – verbally? In writing? Who has this been agreed with?

- Ensuring all the necessary information – who from? Is it up to date? Who needs to have it?

- Needing to talk about contact events and feelings – whose? Who with? When?

- Acknowledging everyone's roles/responsibilities – who needs to be considered? Who should be involved?

- Planning activities – what? When? Where?

- What if . . . ? – potential issues and options

- Working with the reactions of all involved (including children)

- Working with child re: contact/no contact

    Before: fantasies, preparation

    After: feedback, reassessment, future planning

    Without contact: fantasies, reassessment

- Impact on any existing children in family – birth, step, fostered, adopted

- Support/help – if needed, who from?

- Partnership in relation to contact with

    – birth families

    – previous carers

    – social workers

- Renegotiation – who with? How? Recording?

Direct contact: factors for success

Issues for family or group discussion

ADVANTAGES/DRAWBACKS

- What are they?
- Identify in turn for adopters/foster carers, child, and birth families

PLANNING

- Who should be involved?
- How, where and for how long should it take place?
- What if . . . ? – possibilities and options
- Support/help

PREPARATION – How?

- Preparing the child
- Preparing myself
- Preparing my family

FEEDBACK

- Honesty, encouraging, openness, acknowledging own needs/feelings
- Communicating with the child – When? How?
- Assessing the reactions of others involved

ASSESSMENT AND FUTURE PLANNING

- Re-evaluation of direct contact – indicators?
- What are the implications for the child/everyone else involved?
- What needs to be changed?
- How might this be discussed/renegotiated?

• What have I found out about children's needs/feelings in relation to contact?

....
....

• What have I found out about my own feelings? Those of my immediate family? My extended family or support network? Describe below.

....
....

• How far do children's needs and my own conflict? How do I cope with my own/others' feelings?

....
....

• What parenting skills would help me? Discuss or describe any ideas, techniques or skills you have learnt through completing exercises or through general family discussion.

....
....

• What have I found out about contact? What is important about contact? What is the possible range, type, frequency of contact levels with people who may have previously been involved with the child?

....
....

• How do I prepare/plan for contact and what are the time scales involved for the child? What might be the emotional and practical impact on myself and my own family?

....
....

• What do I need to learn? Describe here any gaps in your knowledge, understanding or parenting skills.

....
....

• Points of agreement/difference between applicants and social worker.

....
....

• Areas for further development and training.

....
....
....

Motivation and Expectations

Contents

Essential reading for social workers

Childrens' Perspectives on Families: Joseph Rowntree Research Findings

'Fostering as seen by the carers' children', Part, D. *Adoption & Fostering,* 17 : 2, 1993

Infertility and Adoption, papers published by the Post Adoption Centre

Raphael-Leff J, *Transition to Parenthood – Infertility.*

Cudmore L, *The Impact of Infertility on the Couple Relationship.*

Burnell A, *His, Hers and Theirs – A Post Adoption Perspective on Gender Issues.*

Howe D, *Adopters on Adoption: Reflections on parenthood and children.*
Covers adopters' own experiences, from first wanting to adopt on into the early adulthood of their adopted children. Particularly helpful in identifying the often unexpected later progress of young people, including continuing growth in relationships with adopters. Contains much case study material.

INTRODUCTION

If families are to care successfully on a permanent basis for a child born to someone else, it is essential for them to understand their own hopes and dreams. These will contain expectations both of themselves as parents and of the child they hope for. Families will also have both conscious and unconscious views of their future family life with the new child or sibling group. If such expectations are to be realistic and flexible enough to be able to adapt to a real child in placement, families will need to be able to think carefully beforehand about why they want to undertake the role of a new parent. They should be able to acknowledge and understand also how their immediate family deals with the demands, satisfactions and frustrations of day-by-day life together.

Social workers can find it helpful to bear in mind that many of the possible motivations for caring for a child can support families and encourage them to persist in an often difficult task. What is essential is that motivations are understood and harnessed in the right way i.e. appropriately in relation to the needs of the child. Above all families' motivation must enable them to be able to *accept the child as he or she is*, or within a group of siblings to accept each child for themselves.

Sound preparatory work can help prospective parents identify many of their own motivations, needs and expectations early on. This should lead to better assessment and matching and prepare families to come to terms with the reality of a child placed. The placement will mean coping with the reality of themselves as imperfect parents at the same time as dealing with the many and often potentially overwhelming pressures of caring for a very needy child. After placement, families can only too readily equate their unmet hopes and fantasies with failure either on their part or the child's. Feelings of continuing frustration and failure can be very corrosive elements within a family. They are damaging both to adult and child relationships and ultimately can undermine the stability of the placement itself. Good preparation can, however, help families to develop more realistic expectations before placement. This will enable them to prepare and build effective strategies for handling their own feelings and adapting their family functioning to incorporate a new family member.

The exercises and background reading which follow are all designed to enable families to explore these issues, taking time and care over this vital part of their assessment and, most importantly, sharing feedback with immediate family members who can have very different needs and perspectives. This is a complex area of work and it is important to remember that such exercises cannot be exhaustive in meeting every aspect of particular situations and needs. Social workers should therefore encourage families to raise any other issues which seem particularly relevant for them.

The motivation to parent

Background information for social workers

Info Sheet 1 *Acknowledging the strengths/needs of single carers*

Reading for social workers

Gottman, *Why marriages succeed or fail*
Written for people in permanent relationships and contains much material which could be used directly with applicants including self tests

Owen M, *Novices, Old Hands and Professionals: Adoption by single people*

Hicks S & McDermott J (eds), *Lesbian & Gay Fostering & Adoption: Extraordinary yet ordinary*
Includes accounts by gay men and lesbians, single people and couples, black and white and covers permanent as well as short-term placements.

Reading for applicants

Sparks K, *Why Adoption? Experiences to share for teenagers and their adoptive parents*
An insight into the experience of adoption from a young person's perspective.

'Days of Doubt', *Adoption UK*, May 1995

'From pain comes understanding', *Adoption UK*, February 1994

Applicants reach the stage of enquiry and assessment as prospective parents/carers through adoption and fostering via many different life routes. Enabling them to think about how and why they reached this point in their lives will help them to acknowledge their own needs and feelings, as well as begin to explore how they see themselves fulfilling the role of foster carer or adoptive parent. For some single people or couples who are childless, this may be a relatively unexplored area; for those applicants who already have children, their perception of this new role may be strongly influenced by their previous experiences.

Every prospective parent/carer being prepared and assessed will hold their own particular fantasies of how they will fulfil that new role. They will have not only their visions of success but also the anticipation of how soon they will achieve this – often much more easily and quickly than will be experienced in reality. Knowledge of the extent of children's past hurts may fuel their expectations of "making these better". Thus, awareness of likely difficult behaviour may be mirrored by their anticipation of understanding fully a child's feelings, concerns and needs and being able to reason with them about appropriate ways of expressing these. The more strongly and deeply such parenting fantasies persist, the more difficult it will be for new parents/carers to deal with the many disappointments they will then face. To the reality of the child's complex emotional responses may be added the bitterness of the new parents' ruined expectations.

For all applicants, a continuing personal re-evaluation of what to expect of themselves as well as the child will be essential, informed by a more realistic matching of their preconceptions of parenting with the likely realities of life after placement. Applicants also need to be encouraged to remember there is no such thing as a perfect parent, only a "good enough" one who can admit their faults, learn from their mistakes as well as enjoy their successes, and who constantly tries to improve their skills.

All applicants will need assessment and preparation for their ability to protect children who have been abused. For this aspect of preparation there are some specific materials already in existence (see 'Reading for Applicants' in Section 3). A high proportion of children placed in families will have previously suffered some form of abuse, whether physical, emotional or sexual, although not all such children will have been identified prior to placement. All applicants should therefore receive adequate preparation to recognise any signs of abuse, to be able to deal with their own needs and feelings, and to enable them to respond effectively both to the child and within their family and community network.

Applicants will also need to be helped to develop appropriate "family policies" in order to meet the needs of an abused child while at the same time ensuring that family members are not vulnerable to unfounded allegations of abuse. Issues covered should include who will give personal care to the child, implications for family behaviour and discipline, and how further guidance and support will be ensured both for child and carers. The impact of caring for an abused child on other children in the carer's family should not be ignored or underestimated. This could include, for example, information on physical, emotional or sexual abuse disclosed to another child, bullying behaviour, or involvement in sexualised play. Such events can lead to severe conflicts of responsibilities, loyalties or affection for carers. Strategies for meeting these must be thought about and prepared in advance, including the provision of adequate information and support for existing children in the family as well as therapeutic help for the child placed.

However, social workers also need to remember that, for a small proportion of applicants, there may be child protection issues involved in seeking a child to parent. This possibility should be borne in mind not only at the beginning but also throughout the whole assessment process, irrespective of how the applicants present themselves in terms of social background, class, professional qualifications or experience, etc.

Possible warning signs about applicants may include an apparent need to "control" children's appearance, development or behaviour; attitudes to sexuality which cause concern; or feelings of discomfort about applicants felt by one or more workers, by the group or through referees. It is of the greatest importance that any "funny feelings" should be checked out further during the assessment. As well as the standard agency checks, personal references should always be directly and thoroughly taken up, with specific mention made of potential child protection issues. Good quality supervision, where any anxieties about applicants can be acknowledged and discussed, is vital and further guidance or consultation should also be sought from experienced child protection colleagues if necessary.

Although social workers must remain alert to any warning signs, they also need an awareness that child abusers generally possess very good social skills. Such people will disguise potential signs of abuse or rationalise them extremely well, maintaining a plausibility which can be exceptionally difficult to challenge or expose.

Applicants about whom any concern remains regarding their potential for abusing a child, or failing to protect children from abuse, should be screened out of the assessment process at an early stage where possible, or the worker's concerns made explicit at panel hearing.

Issues for partnerships

Even an exceptionally strong partnership will be tested to its limits when a new child is placed on a permanent basis in the family. Helping couples to explore the dynamics, strengths and any vulnerabilities in their existing relationship will be a prerequisite in any assessment. This will enable them to strengthen their coping strategies further. Alternatively, they might recognise that taking on this new role has the potential to be damaging for themselves and any existing children as well as for the new child.

Gottman suggests that successful marriages are not demonstrated by absence of conflict, or even by its extent, but by how it is handled. Warning signs for potential marital or partnership breakdown may include existing patterns of, or the growth of, criticism, defensiveness, contempt and stonewalling (Gottman, 1997). Such signs may be expressed both verbally and in body language, with growing distancing between partners, intensity and expression of negative feelings, and individual loneliness. The development of parallel and separate life patterns will also emerge. However, his research suggests that nothing foretells a marriage's future as accurately as how a couple retells their past:

> The crucial factor is not necessarily the reality of a marriage's early days but how husband and wife currently view their joint history. When a marriage is unravelling, husband and wife come to recast their earlier times together in a negative light.

Issues for single carers

Single carers may be defined as those who are not in a cohabiting relationship at the time of their application/approval (Owen, 1999). However, they may previously have had long-term relationships and some will have birth children. Despite the fact that single carers have always been eligible to adopt, Owen's study shows that they are likely to feel unsure about their acceptability to agencies, both as single adults and because their material circumstances may be more limited eg. for some applicants from minority ethnic groups. Awareness and sensitivity to this is required, both in planning and running group sessions, and in acknowledging the impact for single applicants of any earlier, as well as post approval, experiences of contact with agencies.

> In one case involving a nine year old girl … 57 families had been considered prior to the selection of the single woman who finally adopted her.   (Owen, 1999).

Stereotypes concerning the homogeneity or support networks of single carers should be avoided. They will come from a wide range of backgrounds and many will have close multi-generational family links, grown-up children outside the household, and a range of close friends they can depend on. Many, once successful

in their application, go on to adopt more than one child, and a new placement appears to be less stressful for existing, as well as newly placed, children in these circumstances.

These placements can, therefore, have many strengths and neither the single status of carers nor their gender or sexuality should be seen as predominant factors within an assessment. The impact of childlessness and where applicable infertility should not, however, be overlooked. Many single carers may also have decided not to take a partner post placement in view of the permanent commitment they are making to the child (Owen, 1999).

a

THINKING ABOUT YOUR MOTIVATION

Identify how many of the possible motivations from the following list apply to each member of your family.

- using existing experience as a parent
- using professional skills (eg. with health needs)
- (for couples) strengthening an existing relationship
- sharing a first child within a new relationship (eg. second marriage)
- infertility
- companionship for an existing child
- filling a family space/"gap" (eg. loss of a previous child, or wanting a large family or a child of one or other sex)
- altruistic needs – feeling you could help by sharing your energies and resources
- overcoming frustrations elsewhere in life (eg. in employment or unemployment)
- "proving" own abilities – either to self or others

- awareness of children's needs (eg. own childhood in care)
- as a result of own childhood experiences (eg. as part of a large sibling group)
- (for existing children) to have a brother or sister, or to please your parents
- seeking a child with high dependency needs (eg. through disability)
- providing a lesbian/gay placement, for example, for a gay/lesbian teenager or if requested
- offering a similar ethnicity, religion, language or culture to a child
- being unemployed and having time/energies to offer something useful
- providing something the community will value
- offering strengths/skills developed from experience of disability

Can you suggest any other motivations relevant for you?

Looking at the above list again, can you see ways in which your motivations could be helpful, or possibly unhelpful, to a child?

b

THE RIVER OF LIFE

Draw a winding river with many bridges and rocks. Ask each adult to describe how they got to the point of wanting to care for a child on a permanent basis. Which of the bridges helped them move forward, and which rocks were barriers to them? Within a family or in a preparation group, discuss the different rivers of life.

c **WANTING TO BE A PARENT**

The following choice of questions to explore can be used with small groups, families, or individual applicants.

- Why do you think your parents had children?

- Why do you want to have children?

- What do you look forward to most as a parent?

- What five things worry you most about being a parent?

- (for couples) Why do you think your partner wants to foster or adopt?

- What would other people (extended family, friends, community) say about your plans?

For children in the family:

- Why do you think your parent/s want/s to foster or adopt?

- What do you look forward to most about having another child in the family? What worries you?

- Who can you talk to about any difficulties?

- What would your friends say about it?

d **ISSUES FOR PARTNERSHIPS**

Questions for partners (both together and separately):

- When, where and how often do you generally discuss things?

- How do you/your partner show caring and appreciation for each other?

- When you feel irritated or frustrated with your partner, how do each of you generally behave?

- How do you know what your partner feels about things?

- When you disagree what do you/your partner do about it?

- What sort of things do you generally do together/apart?

Rewriting history:

Ask the couple to tell you about their courtship, wedding (or deciding to live together) and early days of partnership. Do they:

- Recall their early relationship as chaotic/stressful or as well motivated and happy?

- Look back at earlier difficulties with pride and a sense of joint accomplishment at having overcome them?

- Express a sense of "bonding" while making adjustments to each other?

- Remember specific qualities which attracted them to their partner?

- Express positive feelings when recalling each other at earlier stages of the relationship?

Motivation and Expectations: Module 4 Section 1

Single carers: acknowledging their strengths/needs

POTENTIAL STRENGTHS OF SINGLE CARERS

- Non-stigmatising (about a quarter of all UK families)

- Lack of contradictory adult expectations for child

- Simpler dynamics/negotiation for parent – child relationship

- Absence of inter-adult tensions

- Feeling of safety regarding previous abuse (female carer)

THE NEEDS OF SINGLE CARERS

- Positive recruitment and clear messages

- To be helped to not feel "less eligible"

- Assessment focused on parenting potential not on single carer status

- Recognition of experiences of infertility

- To have their particular strengths clearly identified/acknowledged

- Identification of full potential as carers for a range of children

Expectations of children

Reading for applicants

Wilson J, *The Story of Tracy Beaker*
The fictional story of a 10-year-old girl who, despite previous fostering disruptions, would like to leave her children's home to live in a family. A beautifully observed, touching and often very funny tale, all told in Tracy's own words. Could be enjoyed also by older children.

Each family will be continuing to think and learn during the process of assessment about the sort of child they feel they can most successfully care for. Some characteristics such as age, number of children or gender may be more easily explored than others, they may not even be consciously aware of their own expectations of the child they hope to parent, let alone have shared these with other members of their family or with you as the social worker undertaking the assessment.

These expectations may revolve around aspects such as appearance, personality and their potential achievements. For example, their conscious or unconscious feelings about their child's appearance are likely to impinge on early responses to visual information such as photographs. Such responses are vital clues to how far a family will be able to accept the child for who they are, and it is important to remember also that family members may have different responses and that it is essential to enable them to share and discuss these at the earliest possible stage.

The same issues will apply in relation to the behaviour which can either be tolerated by families, or which they seek to improve or build on in the child's development. In relation to the child's potential achievements, families may have expectations about their education, their sporting abilities, their shared interests with family members or their emotional development (eg. perhaps that they will become a full and committed family member).

It is vital and helpful for families to acknowledge the existence of the "fantasy child" who is likely to have a great bearing on the success or otherwise of an eventual placement. Unmet needs or unfulfilled expectations relating to "fantasy children" sadly often feature in disruption meetings when a hoped for permanent placement has come to an end. An awareness of these long before matching or placement takes place will help families in achieving a successful placement.

a

WHAT AM I HOPING FOR? –
ACHIEVEMENTS AND DISAPPOINTMENTS

This exercise can be used for group work

1. Make up a set of cards (for some suggestions, see overleaf) adding to and adapting these as appropriate for disability, gender, ethnicity, etc. Depict the following continuum on either a large table or the floor.

Achievement	Disappointment
Positive feeling	Negative feeling

Each participant is given a couple of cards and decides personally for themselves where they will place their cards, as a starting point, on the continuum and say why they have placed them there. The mid-point of the continuum line is where they would have no strong feelings either way. Participants then take it in turn to place their cards.

Invite comments from the rest of the group – where do they feel the card should be placed and why? Participants who want to move someone else's card have to negotiate with the person who put it down before doing so. Remember to give permission for views to be changed or altered as the exercise progresses.

Facilitators need to prompt discussion regarding feelings/expectations if the situations stay the same or change as the adoptive placement progresses.

Gather in the cards and share with families the reality of some of the children who are waiting for a placement (e.g. using *Be My Parent* and photos/information about the agency's own children).

b

WHAT IS THE CHILD LIKE?

Can be used for small group work or for a family with existing children.

Give everyone a stick figure that represents the child they have in mind (or figures if they are seeking a sibling group). Ask them to think about and then describe the following (in writing and/or verbally):

- Who is the child? Their family?

- Why is he or she in care?

- What is the child like (appearance, development, abilities, personality, needs)?

What am I hoping for

To be used with Exercise a

CARD EXAMPLES

Child has plenty of friends and is often invited to birthday parties

Child has no friends – teacher says he/she is 'just a loner'

Despite drama lessons child remains painfully shy and unassertive

Child aged 12 hates family weekend camping trips and refuses to go

Child attached to parent but continually picks on adoptive sibling

Child shows no interest in parents' jobs or hobbies

Child helps parent complete birthday cake for aunt

Child talks openly about fears to mother

Child loves going to football match with father

Child writes in diary and locks it up – won't talk about feelings

Child always falling out with friends

Child insists on telling all friends and visitors that they were adopted

Child insists on keeping picture of birth mother on wall

Child quickly calls parent/s 'mum' and/or 'dad'

Child becomes closer friend with siblings

Child stops talking about birth family

Child very good at sport but not at school work

Child says he thinks he is gay

Child develops depression

Child loves being comforted

Child wets the bed at 10 years of age

Child won't give up bottle at age 4

Child reads by age 4

Child aged 9 is able to attend mainstream school

Child aged 10 years still needs extra classroom help in primary school

Child catches up educationally – passes SATS

11-year-old boy suspended for pushing a teacher

Child fails entrance exam to chosen secondary school

Child fails all GCSEs and wants to leave school

Child joins school choir and is selected for school play

Child aged 13 needs remedial lessons in reading

Child aged 8 is identified as dyslexic

16-year-old wants to leave school and learn to be a bricklayer

Child aged 6 attending mainstream school is identified as needing special education

Child aged 10 bites another child in playground

Child aged 15 wants to go to university

Child aged 12 truants from school

Child aged 9 won't join cubs or brownies

Family are all keen swimmers but child refuses to learn

Child has no hobbies

Child wins prize in art competition

Child wants to get a paper round

Child only interested in expensive possessions

Child refuses to attend church

Child is caring towards siblings

Child is only interested in speaking English and not her/his first language

Child enjoys attending traditional cultural events

c

CHILDREN'S NEEDS – BEING CLEAR ABOUT WHAT YOU CAN CONSIDER

To help applicants identify both potential "coping" and "no go" areas for them. The exercise can be completed either with the family at home or in a group meeting, using Information Sheets 3 to 6.

The social worker should consider in advance the following questions:

- Are the circles shown appropriate/sufficient for the family or group being prepared/assessed?

- How can the possibilities outlined be prevented from seeming overwhelming to families?

Ask the applicants to look at the possible needs children may have within each of the following four areas: (see Information Sheets 3 to 6)

- The emotional impact of separation and loss
- The effects of poor early attachment patterns
- Possible results of sexual abuse or inappropriate sexual knowledge
- Acceptance of background factors

For each worksheet:

i) Colour in each circle as follows:

- Green for needs applicants are confident they can work with.
- Red for needs applicants are very clear they could not/would not want to cope with
- Orange for needs applicants are uncertain about, but may be able to meet with further help.

ii) Ask applicants to talk about their selections and any particular issues they have identified. How do different members of the family feel?

d

THE CHILD IN YOUR FAMILY

Use experienced adopters to present this exercise with you, and then to share their experiences of reality with applicants. How do applicants feel about these? (Remember, this can be a powerful exercise and applicants will need support.)

Visualise your "fantasy child" in one or more of the following situations, and add others as appropriate:

- When you are sharing a meal

- At a family event eg. a child's birthday party or a family wedding

- When he or she is disappointed and angry

- When you are in the supermarket

- When you are ill or busy and cannot give him/her any attention

- At school
    – in the classroom
    – in the playground

What are they doing?
How do they appear – to yourself and others?
How do you feel about them?

The implications of emotional damage to children

ISSUES TO DISCUSS IN A FAMILY OR GROUP

Consider what children may bring with them, adding to the examples given. What does this mean for the family's expectations of children placed? How far can families adapt their expectations and what will help them in this task?

CHILDREN'S PERCEPTIONS OF

Carers : Bringing experiences of inappropriate or abusive care in previous families

Themselves: eg. as scapegoat, useless at school, as primary carer for siblings

Family life: eg. may manipulate others; avoid notice or seek constant attention; expect criticism rather than praise

CHILDREN'S FEELINGS

May have limited/no ability to show feelings, either about self or others.

Still has to learn how to recognise feelings and how/why these develop.

Child's lack of resources (ie. vocabulary to talk about feelings and how to express them appropriately)

Child cannot accept/cope with negative feelings

Child's feelings from past not dealt with (eg. grief, anger or fear)

CHILDREN'S BEHAVIOUR

Child expresses needs and feelings inappropriately or hides them

Behaviour is often inappropriate/unhelpful/challenging

Child continues learnt patterns of behaviour from the past

May seek a means of communication but needs help with developing this

CHILDREN'S RELATIONSHIPS

Child has poor understanding of how relationships work

Displays negative skills in relating to adults and/or other children, eg. disruptive, aggressive

Early environment leads child to expect failure – limits motivation to achieve

Child can undermine family functioning/adult partnerships/social networks

Child cannot offer mutuality, sharing or reciprocate to others

Child may resist/fear closeness, intimacy, or caring from adults.

Kunstal, adapted from Mending Fractured Lives, workshop material

Possible effects of separation and loss

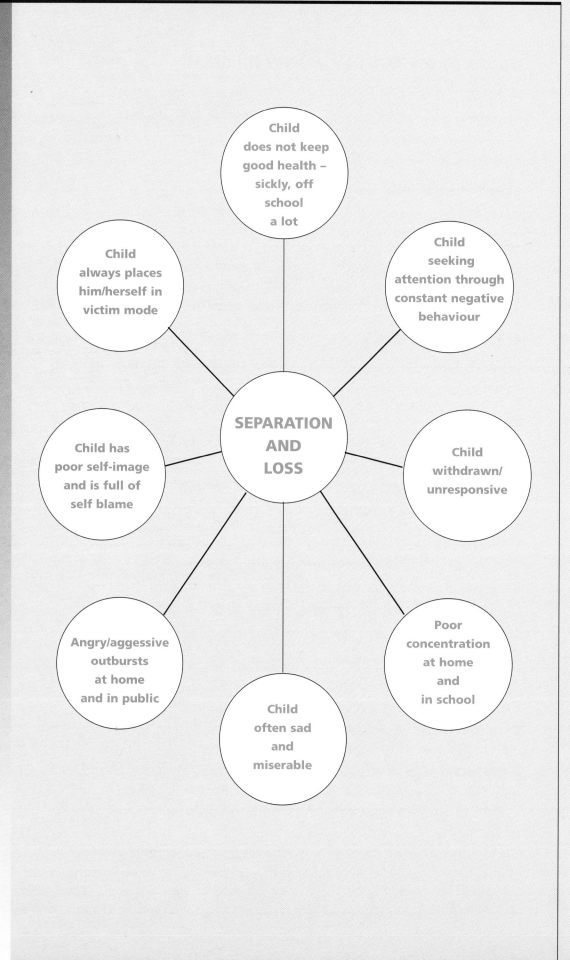

Child does not keep good health – sickly, off school a lot

Child always places him/herself in victim mode

Child seeking attention through constant negative behaviour

SEPARATION AND LOSS

Child has poor self-image and is full of self blame

Child withdrawn/ unresponsive

Angry/aggressive outbursts at home and in public

Child often sad and miserable

Poor concentration at home and in school

Possible effects of poor early attachment experiences

Child doesn't understand what makes things happen, confused between fact and fantasy

Child has learning problems at school – blocks and gaps

Child has eating problems eg. chewing solids, storing food under bed, doesn't know when full, can't eat meals but just snacks all the time

Child anxiously attached-clingy

Child makes superficial attachment – can't get close

Child has problems making/keeping friends in own peer group

Child asks incessant questions which are often nonsense

Child indiscriminately affectionate with strangers

EARLY ATTACHMENT ISSUES

Child steals from shops

Child has speech problems – reverts to baby talk

Child prone to severe temper tantrums

Child has limited conscience development; needs an adult to tell him/her what is right and wrong

Child poorly physically co-ordinated – accident prone

Child cruel to animals

Child inflicts self-harm eg. head banging, biting inside of mouth, picking blemishes on skin

Child steals fom family

Child destructive of own and other people's material things

Child steals fom school

Child tells lies, not to get out of things but even when caught in the act

Child hyperactive, has sleeping problems eg. eneuretic

Possible effects of sexual abuse

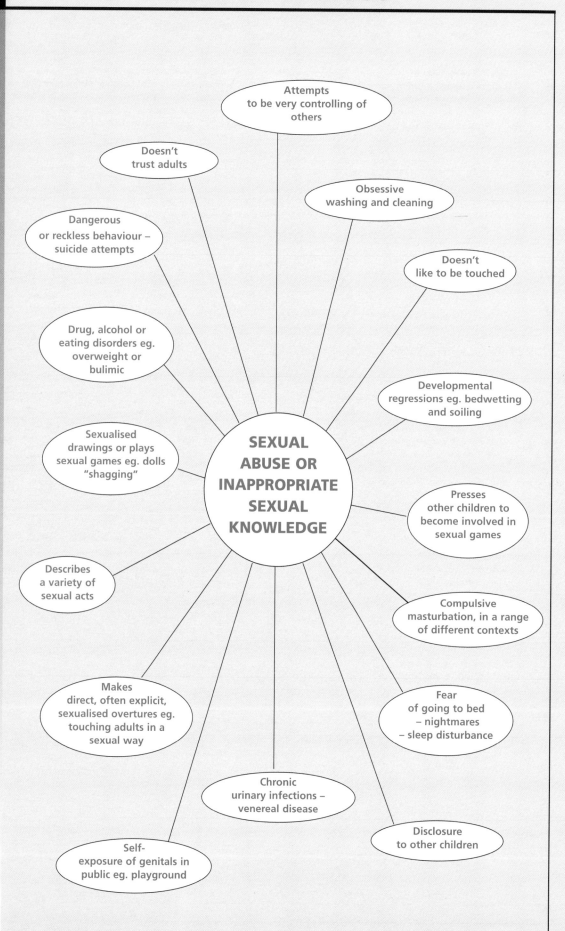

SEXUAL ABUSE OR INAPPROPRIATE SEXUAL KNOWLEDGE

Attempts to be very controlling of others

Doesn't trust adults

Obsessive washing and cleaning

Dangerous or reckless behaviour – suicide attempts

Doesn't like to be touched

Drug, alcohol or eating disorders eg. overweight or bulimic

Developmental regressions eg. bedwetting and soiling

Sexualised drawings or plays sexual games eg. dolls "shagging"

Presses other children to become involved in sexual games

Describes a variety of sexual acts

Compulsive masturbation, in a range of different contexts

Makes direct, often explicit, sexualised overtures eg. touching adults in a sexual way

Fear of going to bed – nightmares – sleep disturbance

Chronic urinary infections – venereal disease

Disclosure to other children

Self-exposure of genitals in public eg. playground

Acceptance of background factors

Child with a genetic risk eg. epilepsy

Child born of an incestuous relationship

Child whose mother was drinking heavily during the pregnancy and may suffer foetal alcohol effect

Child whose birth father is in prison for theft and violent offences

Sibling group who all have different birth fathers

Child whose birth parents are alcoholics or drug users

Child with siblings who have learning disabilities

ACCEPTANCE OF BACKGROUND FACTORS

Child where nothing is known about the birth father

Child with parent who has learning difficulties

Child whose birth mother is a prostitute

Child whose birth mother is an intravenous drug user with an increased risk of HIV/AIDS for the child

Child with schizophrenia in birth parent

Child born with a severe learning and/or physical disability

Child from a travelling family

Child with special education needs

Child at tisk of hepatitis

MODULE 4

Functioning as a family before placement

Background information for social workers

■ *Family Talk*
A picture pack, suitable for use with children aged between about six and eleven. Designed to help children talk about family life and understand the implications of a new brother or sister joining their family.

Reading for social workers

■ 'Fatherhood, Fathering & Adoption', *Adoption UK,* May 1995

Reading for applicants

■ 'Fatherhood, Fathering & Adoption', *Adoption UK,* May 1995

■ 'The Right Moment has Gone', *Adoption UK*, November 1996
Covers issues related to the needs of the birth child.

■ *Safe Caring*, NFCA
Provides practical advice for carers on how to look after children who have been or may have been sexually abused. Helps carers to develop a "family policy" on matters such as who gives a child personal care, being open and honest about sharing information, and supervising children's play.

■ Smith G, *The Protector's Handbook*
Gives adults the vital information and skills needed to protect children in their day-to-day lives. Includes recognising the signs of abuse and its emotional effects on children, as well as suggesting strategies and resources for responding effectively.

Existing family life patterns and roles may not be set in stone but there will be a solidity and implicit level of understanding about these between family members which will have built up throughout the family's life together. It will take a long time before such a detailed level of understanding is reached by a child or sibling group coming into a new family. In every family, existing patterns will also need to change to make space for a new child's development, needs and personality.

Each family's way of coping with everyday life is unique, shaped by cultural and sometimes also religious patterns, as well as the personalities and previous experiences of each family member. Issues such as "race", class, gender, economic power, age or any disability also play an important part in family life. Potential new parents/carers need to develop their conscious understanding of how their own family functions and how each individual role interacts. They will then be able to explain these to a new child, adapt family patterns where necessary, and guide the child successfully through the many currents and ups and downs of family existence. Particularly important is the consideration of potential relationships with any existing children in the family and how these may be successfully developed and everyone's needs fully considered.

Expectations and patterns of how sex and sexuality are dealt with in the new parent/carer's family life will be extremely significant for any child placed.

> *Long before children enter school their gender, identity and feelings about sexuality have been shaped by their early experiences with family members.* (Fahlberg, 1994)

The way in which the new permanent family deals with issues of sexuality, including the level of its understanding and expectations of "normal" sexual development, will therefore play a crucial role in how well it can care for a child who may have had years of disrupted or inappropriate upbringing before this placement.

Feelings of adults about their own sexuality and gender, and how well or otherwise they were

Further reading for social workers

◼ Fahlberg, V *A Child's Journey through Placement*.
Chapter 2 deals extensively with the developing sexuality of children and young people.

◼ Brodzinsky D and Schechter M (eds), *The Psychology of Adoption*.
Chapter 3 – 'Adoption from the inside out: A psychoanalytic perspective' and Chapter 7 – 'Acknowledgement or rejection of differences?'

◼ Rosenberg E B, *The Adoption Life Cycle*.
Chapter 3: 'Becoming parents/developmental tasks: phases 1-3'.

◼ Reich D, 'Family Creation: The continuing impact of infertility' in *Infertility & Adoption*.

◼ BAAF: *Effective Panels*.
Chapter 5: Families offering placements.

◼ Clulow C (Ed), *Partners Becoming Parents*.
A study of adapting to the birth of a baby but contains much relevant material on assessing the functioning of partnerships and improving adaptation to caring for a child

taught to acknowledge, understand and deal with these in childhood and while growing up will be significant, and will impact on how well they can help the child with issues about sex and sexuality. These will include issues arising from any sexual abuse and its serious implications not only for the child's development but for family life in general. Applicants will also need to develop a sound knowledge of the physical and psychological changes and range of "normal" behaviours related to childhood and adolescent sexuality. They will need to demonstrate that they feel comfortable about accepting and handling these, and that they will be able to provide both information and guidance on decision making and values related to sexuality, making this appropriate to the age and developmental stage of children and young people, including those with a disability.

a

FAMILY DYNAMICS AND PERSONALITIES

For a family group, including any children.

Part 1. Think (individually) about what your own family is like eg. whether family members are physically affectionate, volatile, persevering, like/dislike routine. Then identify (again individually) which sort of animal would best represent your family and say why.

Part 2. Which animals best represent each of you individually and why?

How did the animals represent how each person is alike/different?

Part 3. What were the differences in the way each of you saw your family?

b

FAMILY RULES AND ROUTINES

Can be used with a family or for small group work.

What would a child need to know about your family? Make a "family brick" (on paper) for each factor identified.

Which three bricks would be the most important initially?

Compare differences/similarities either within the family or group.

c

OFFERING A PLACEMENT/FINDING A MATCH

For small group work

Make up two sets of different coloured cards, one representing families and the other children. The family cards show a family's wishes for the sort of child they are seeking. The children's cards show their characteristics and needs (age, gender, "race", disability, sibling group, emotional and behavioural needs, etc)

Distribute an equal number of family or children's cards. Ask participants to think about the description on their cards, then if they have a child's card to talk to others holding family cards, and vice versa to try and find an appropriate match. Arrange that some cards do not match up.

Ask applicants:

- What they learnt about the needs of children and families
- How they found the process.

For suggestions for possible cards, see overleaf and adapt as necessary for your particular group.

Offering a placement/finding a match

Examples of possible cards

PARENTS

Can adopt a child with disabilities who will be able to live independently as an adult.

We are a white English couple in our mid 30s. We want to adopt a sibling group with at least one child under five.

We are a black African-Caribbean couple in our mid 30s. We want to adopt a sibling group of two or three children.

Can care for a child who has been sexually abused.

Can care for a child with a terminal illness.

Can accept a child placed having letterbox contact with birth parent/s.

Can provide a loving home for a child who has special educational needs.

We are experienced in special education teaching. We can provide a loving home for a child (either sex) nine years old or under. Child must be in mainstream education.

Can take a child (preferably a girl) up to the age of eight. My partner and I are not able to have our own children.

I am an Asian woman and my partner is white. We want a child of mixed parentage as young as possible.

Can take a child/ren who has contact with siblings but not birth parents.

Offering a placement/finding a match

Examples of possible cards

CHILDREN

I am a 13-year-old boy with cerebral palsy. I want to work with computers when I am grown up. I need a family who can help me achieve this.

I need a family who can adopt me (nine) and my brother (seven) and sister (four). My brother has a learning disability.

I need a family who can adopt me and my brother. Our mum is white and my dad is white and my brother's dad is Jamaican.

I have been sexually abused and I want to live with just a female carer.

I am a baby who was born HIV positive. I may develop AIDS. My agency wants a family to adopt me.

I want a family to adopt me but I also want face-to-face contact with my mum and uncle.

I am a 10-year-old girl. I go to a special school because I have a learning disability. I want a family with a dog, who will care for me permanently.

I am an eight-year-old boy who goes to a special school for kids with emotional and behavioural difficulties. I want a family to adopt me.

I am a seven-year-old boy. I have lived in five different families since coming into care. My social worker wants to find a new family for me but I'm not sure.

I am a two-year-old mixed parentage child (Asian Moslem/white). My mother wants me to be raised in the Islamic faith.

We want a family who will help us to keep in touch with our older sister who is fostered and our younger brother who still lives at home.

Learning points about motivation and expectations

- What have I found out about children's needs/feelings?

....

....

- What have I found out about my own motivation/functioning/expectations? Those of my immediate family? Describe below.

....

....

- What might be helpful/unhelpful to me in caring for a child?

....

....

- What parenting skills would help me? (eg. ability to see and accept the child as they are/able to understand and convey family roles and rules) Add any others that you can think of.

....

....

- How do I cope with my own/others motives or expectations? Discuss or describe any ideas, techniques or skills you have learnt through completing exercises or through general family discussion.

....

....

- Are there any limitations in my own family's self-awareness and understanding of each other and our family rules which we need to work on?

....

....

- Points of agreement/difference between applicants and social worker

....

....

- Areas identified for future development/training

....

....

....

Impact, Survival and Growth

Contents

Essential reading for social workers

INTRODUCTION

Increasing the size of an alternative family through adoption or fostering means not only making the many adjustments to family life needed at the time of placement, but also coping with the continuing impact over many years of meeting the needs of a vulnerable, and often emotionally disturbed, child or sibling group.

Achieving a much hoped for placement can become the family's primary aim after a period of enquiry, application and assessment which can appear unnecessarily intrusive and long drawn out. However, the start of a placement is only the beginning of the lifetime tasks involved. In their future role, alternative families will need to fulfil successfully a series of additional parenting tasks for a child who has suffered early separation and loss and who is being brought up outside his or her birth family. Many of the issues explored within the earlier modules such as attachment and identity will continue to play themselves out throughout life as the adopted or fostered child reaches every new developmental stage, or faces a major change of family circumstances such as moving house or school or the serious illness of a parent/carer.

Parenting is a life-time relationship with the child and needs coping strategies to reflect this. These will change over the family's life cycle in order to adapt and meet the child's needs not only throughout childhood but as he or she becomes an adult. Being helped at an early stage of preparation and assessment to acknowledge and consider this helps families to lay the necessary strong foundations. Building on these they can continue to grow in their capacities and be enabled to care appropriately and effectively over the years ahead.

Dealing with both the short and long-term impact of placement on all family members including any existing children will enable the family to build both skills and confidence in approaching future issues. Families will need to develop an appreciation of the developmental life time tasks involved for the adoptees and the birth parents as well as themselves (Rosenberg, 1992) if they are to handle the future complexities and impact of the placement successfully (for Lifetime Tasks for Adoptees, see Module 2, *Identity*). The child's siblings (as identified by the child him/herself) will also generally be of increasing significance in later life, offering the longest lifetime relationships available to the child. The availability and understanding offered by the family's support network will play a crucial role throughout in helping the family cope with the challenges and ongoing demands of the placement and both personal and professional support should be available to the family.

Sadly, though, however carefully the assessment and preparation are undertaken and however positively the placement commences and is supported, some placement disruptions will inevitably take place over future years. Within these destabilising and painful situations the child's needs must be prioritised and protected. Anticipation of such possibilities in advance will help the family cope better at that time in keeping the child's needs centre stage.

Building resilience in children

Background information for social workers

Info Sheet 1 *Protective factors for psychological resilience*

Info Sheet 2 *Helping children move into permanent placement – the family's role*

Reading for applicants

'Living in Hope', *Adoption UK*, November 1996.
The long- term issues arising in baby placements

Argent H, *Whatever happened to Adam?*
Follows the outcomes into adulthood of young people with disabilities placed in alternative families.

McNamara J, *Bruised before Birth*
Considers the social and behavioural development of children exposed to parental substance abuse, but contains many practical tools and suggestions for resources to help any child cope with change, stress and difficulties in communication or learning. See particularly Chapters 3, 4 and 5.

For children to have the best chance of thriving (or at times even surviving) permanent placement is the essential foundation on which progress is built. It is not an end in itself. A wide supportive environment/network including the permanent family, their extended family, school, and all community links working well together give a child maximum opportunities to reach developmental milestones. The type and degree of support children need will depend on the quality and extent of preparatory work done with them and their own previous unique experiences of care and relationships.

Both children and families will need to develop resilience in handling ever-changing needs arising from the placement and in using their experiences to improve coping skills for the future. Skills in dealing with both family and external environments such as the school and community will be important. Building family skills can be addressed both throughout the preparation for a placement and in ongoing training and support subsequently. Development of children's skills and resilience may receive less specific attention but is an important task for their alternative families. Successfully managing the child's initial transition into the family is crucial but children will also need increasing opportunities to develop the "building blocks" of resilience (Gilligan, 1997). These include a secure base, self-esteem and an internal sense of competence to know how to cope with the world.

For black children and those from minority ethnic groups and for children with disabilities there will be particular issues of racism or discrimination to face throughout their lives (see also Module 3, *Identity*). For all children, setting a series of appropriate and achievable goals throughout childhood and adolescence and supporting them in achieving these will enable children to taste success and reinforce their wish to achieve, to handle disappointment and to learn from their mistakes. In this way they will gradually build up their resilience and the skills they need for adulthood.

Providing a secure base

A secure base is one which 'encourages and renders safe exploration of the wider world' (Bowlby, 1988). Providing a secure base and a feeling of belonging is a major reason for seeking permanence for children. Such a base will meet a child's fundamental need to be part of a family to which he or she feels able to return into early adulthood and beyond at times of distress or practical difficulties, as well as to share their experiences of happiness and success.

A secure base for the child should, in time, include rewarding and supportive relationships at school or work, in social or recreational activities, and through the availability of professional help as well as from the child's permanent family (Gilligan, 1997). Nevertheless, it is within the family rather than in outside and often new networks, that the child's feelings of safety, security and self-confidence should be able most effectively and lastingly to take root and be cultivated. It is important to remember also not to focus entirely on adult–child relationships as the source of emotional strength and security to the child. Other children within the new family, and pets as well, may play a highly significant role while apparently making fewer emotional demands on a child who may not feel ready to consider trusting adults.

The new family will need understanding and skills to develop a child's ability to use their family as a secure base both now and in the future. Carers must start with recognising and addressing the numerous and often previously unrecognised hopes and fears the child will bring into this new placement. This means developing insight into the child's perspectives and ways of thinking as well as accepting a child's past. In this way the child can be appropriately helped to develop the ability to acknowledge and work through his or her feelings of confusion, anger, etc. This process is an essential prerequisite to a child indicating the first tentative feelings of trust and security within their new family environment. However, the family will also need to recognise that with some children progress may appear painfully slow, often patchy and at times non-existent. They may only know

what degree of success they have achieved in establishing the child's ability to accept and use this family as a secure base once adulthood is finally reached. This has been the finding of many experienced carers/parents where a level of maturity and wisdom has finally developed in a young adult despite perhaps a turbulent adolescence (Howe, 1996).

From the very beginning of a placement each permanent family will also need to establish and share fully with the child and all other family members their own particular guidelines for general safety and well being, including safe caring. However, it will be equally important for them to consider within every area of the child's life what degree of risk-taking by children will be encouraged or allowed, and how children can be helped to take responsibility, ask for help when needed, and cope with their mistakes. In certain circumstances families will need to consider what is appropriate in relation to a particular child's history and previous experiences, particularly where there has been abuse or discrimination or where the child has any disabilities. Families also need to be able to adapt guidelines over time to meet a child's growing feelings of security or developmental change. Encourage families to think, for example, about how they will work with a child to encourage and facilitate an appropriate degree of independence, or to address emerging sexual needs including those of young people with a disability.

Sense of competence

Building skills in self-awareness and self care will help children in both expressing their needs and feeling more confident in handling some of these appropriately for themselves. This will enable the family to direct more of their own energies into productively guiding, supporting and facilitating the child's development rather than simply struggling to maintain a difficult status quo. Many children in care are not even well attuned to recognising or handling their own basic physical needs such as feeling cold, hunger or pain.

Children also need to be able to believe in their own ability to improve their situation thus developing a sense of competence (Gilligan, 1997). This can only happen when they possess a repertoire built up from their own experience of successful problem-solving approaches. They may learn these either through teaching by carers or significant adults, or from observation of either adults or peers.

The relationship between a child's chronological and developmental age is also an important factor in developing resilience and can be very variable. It is important for families to be able to look beyond chronological age and see and accept the child as he or she really is. This will include acknowledging all the life skills which are missing because of adverse or inadequate early experiences. Such gaps or limitations in the child's development will impact on his or her life both within the family and outside it. Poor relationships with their peers are frequently a significant problem for fostered or adopted children. In all areas of their development such children are likely to require additional opportunities for role modelling, experimenting, regressing, etc.

Exercises for applicants

CHILDREN'S SELF-AWARENESS

Ask adults to think about an occasion in childhood when they experienced fear, illness, pain, hunger, or danger.

- Who or what helped?

- How could they develop the child's self-awareness, and their ability to be open with carers about physical needs or feelings?

OR

(ii)) Prepare a mobile or simple jigsaw cut from a family photograph with sufficient parts to represent each existing family member. Now ask them to add another figure of a child to represent the new child/children.

- What happens to the balance or the shape of the jigsaw? How might the mobile be rebalanced or a new jigsaw be formed?

- How might the child feel/react during this process?

b **MOVING INTO THE FAMILY**

(i) Ask the family (adult/s and any existing children) to sculpt the new child/children moving towards and into the family group.

- What happens and what are their feelings and those of the child? How could it be managed better?

c **PROVIDING A SECURE BASE**

Ask applicants to consider and discuss the following:

- When did you feel most secure in your childhood and what made it secure? What do you think will be the same/different for a child placed?

- What helped you to become independent and how did you define this? What do you think will be the same/different for a child placed?

- Imagine that the child placed with you is now 17 years old.

  What a) practical and b) emotional resources would you help them build up during their childhood in order to help cope as young adults?

d **COPING SKILLS**

Write down two or three of your own worst experiences as a child. Who or what helped you cope?

- What might have helped you avoid these situations in the first place – or helped you cope better?

- What do you think might be the most difficult new experiences for a child joining your family? (Consider situations both inside and outside the family.) How would you help them cope? Who else might be encouraged to help?

Protective factors
for psychological resilience

Individual

- Social competence
- Intelligence
- Temperamental style
- Problem-solving skills
- Attractiveness
- Ability to organise one's thinking
- Sense of humour
- Developing a coherent life story
- Individual autonomy
- Sense of purpose and future

Social

- Strong sense of community
- Family support
  - high levels of warmth, praise, encouragement
  - low levels of criticism
- Participation in community activities including school life, religious or other affiliation groups
- Child's participation encouraged
- Friendships – in particular a close confiding other
- High expectations
- Positive and secure attachments

Gerrilyn Smith, Clinical Psychologist

Questions for families/groups to discuss

- Which protective factors could you develop for a child? And how might you do this?
- What could be barriers to achieving this?
- Which protective factors would you prioritise?

Helping children move into permanent placement – the family's role

Explanations

- Reinforce what permanence is for them and the child
- Confirm purpose of introductions
- Clarify process of introductions/practicalities/feedback

Seeking information from the child

- Acknowledging child's needs re: timing
- Acceptance of losses for child/help with anxieties
- Welcome child's view of past and future
- Identify likes, dislikes, fears, hopes

Providing information for the child

Identifying child's needs over and above:

- New family/way of life
- New house/community
- New school (and when)
- Help for child with external lifestory
- Contact/no contact provisions

Preparing support for the child

- Other children in the family
  - Extended family/friends
  - Continuity or changes, for example, pets
  - Teachers/peers at school

Family perspectives on survival

Background information for social workers

Info Sheet 3

Life cycle tasks for adopters
Building on/adapting this material, consider also Life Cycle Tasks for Foster Carers offering permanence.

Info Sheet 4

Meeting the needs of children who foster
Building on this material, consider also the relevance of the issues addressed for existing children within adoptive families.

Video

Children Who Foster, obtainable from NFCA
Children of foster families talk about how it feels when your parents are foster carers, and describe both their relationships with the children placed and some of their experiences.

Reading for applicants

■ 'Looking After Number One',
Adoption UK, November 1994

■ Bayard R T & Bayard J, *Help – I've got a teenager, a survival guide for desperate parents*

■ Bearman F, *Surviving Five*
Takes readers through the placement of a large sibling group from introductions to the granting of the adoption order. Covers issues such as "testing out" at home, difficulties at school, and the impact of the placement on an existing child. Describes the rivalries and bonds between the siblings.

Parenting means families thinking about and planning for all the long-term implications of placement including changes in both their and the child's lifecycle. For example, some families may have to face the breakdown of an existing relationship or the illness and death of their own parents at the same time as the adolescence of a child who has been placed. Key stages may also include the child's transition to independent living or the implications of renewing direct contact with their birth parents in young adulthood. The alternative family will, over time, be called upon to renew its role as a result of an adopted or foster child's life cycle changes, and to face additional emotional demands arising from these.

The family will need to strike a careful and sensitive balance between what individual members can contribute to caring for a new child or children and what each of them will need in terms of their own personal rewards and support. The impact of the child will also spread out in ripples beyond the immediate family into their extended family and the wider community. Any resulting frustrations, concerns or decisions taken by others about the new child's needs or behaviour will also inevitably impinge on the family itself.

Developing the family's own resilience to cope with the long-term stresses and strains as well as the pleasures of any placement is essential. Ensure that families think about what would be the hardest pressures for them to cope with e.g. loss of time, lack of any perceptible progress, lack of emotional feedback from the child, pressures on their relationship with partners, negative impact on existing children or critical reactions from extended family or neighbours. Exploration of how they could reduce or handle these will help families understand the strains better and enable them to develop their contingency planning. Families also need to balance all the pressures with their own need to recognise "rewards" from the placement. What rewards are they hoping for? How will they measure success? What will help them keep going if no "normal" rewards are forthcoming?

Exercises for applicants

a. TIME PATTERNS (for each family member)

A particularly useful exercise for childless families but also helpful for busy families with existing children to consider the impact on their present pattern of family life.

- Draw two circles of 24 hours each. In the first one show how your time/energies are split now e.g. immediate family/work/leisure/extended family. In the second one show how you think this would be different after placement.

- Discuss whether other members of your family see either present patterns or the changes differently. Who will be making the greatest adjustments?

c. THE IMPACT ON APPLICANT/S

- How do you think the child will change things in your life?
  What do you feel they will change?

- Identify what "triggers" get to you and make you really angry.
  What helps most (and least) in helping you deal with these?

For couples complete individually, then repeat exercise on partner's behalf and compare lists. For larger family units use indirect/circular questions eg ask Dad, 'What do you think Mum/son/daughter is looking forward to/fearing most about a new child joining the family?'. Repeat for all and check out different perceptions.

b. THE IMPACT ON EXISTING CHILDREN

Part 1

Choose one or more of the following scenarios:

- You have a child aged eight who is being severely bullied by the younger six-year-old placed. How might you realise this? What would you feel/do (including what you would say to both children)? Who might help you?

- You have two children aged 11 and 9 years, who are told by the six-year-old placed (with details) that they have been sexually abused before placement. What do you feel/do? Who might help you?

- You have a son aged 14. Your son is accused by the six-year-old of physical abuse. What do you feel/do? Who might help you?

Part 2

Considering the children from the previous exercise imagine that the birth child/children comes to see you to say that he/she has become increasingly unhappy during the last three months. (The placement took place . . . months/years ago.) You are always 'tired and cross' and 'never have any time for them anymore'. You have also received a lot of negative comment from neighbours, friends and at school about the new child's behaviour. You know that you have been under a lot of pressure but this feels like the "last straw". What do you do?

Part 3

Thinking about the examples above and any others that you might identify, how could any of these situations be either prevented or planned for in advance?

Life cycle tasks for adopters

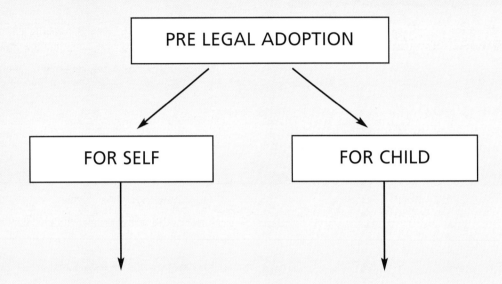

PRE LEGAL ADOPTION

FOR SELF

FOR CHILD

FOR SELF

- Accepting differences with biological parenting

- Accepting birth family links (psychological and physical)

- Developing/strengthening an existing partnership

- Identifying adaptations needed in own family

- Preparing existing children in family and other extended family

- Setting realistic and flexible expectations of self as parents

- Extending appropriate support network for new task

FOR CHILD

- Process of introductions

- Accepting child as he or she is

- Building on previous attachments for child

- Beginning to inform child about adoptive family

- Setting reasonable but positive expectations of child

- Seeking resources in community, for example, education, health, leisure

Life cycle tasks for adopters

FOR SELF	DURING ADOPTION (CHILDHOOD)	FOR CHILD/ YOUNG PERSON

WITH PRESCHOOL CHILDREN

- Acknowledging and valuing adoption

- Revising expectations of self as parents

- Telling the child about adoption

- Creating "external" life story

WITH SCHOOL AGE CHILD

- Supporting valuable birth family links

- Dealing with adoption in extended family/ friendship network

- Dealing with adoption issues in school and wider community

- Dealing with continuous testing out of status and permanence

- Continuing integration as family member

- Maintaining sexual boundaries without incest taboo

WITH ADOLESCENT

- Dealing with own fears/ anxieties about child's development and/or biological links

- Accepting psychological non-genetic model of family

- Accepting and helping young people integrate adoptive/ biological identity

- Helping separation process as teenager

- Helping child with any contact issues

- Facilitating competence skills

- Encouraging wider support network

Impact, Survival and Growth: Module 5 Introduction

Life cycle tasks for adopters

```
        ┌──────────────────────────┐
        │   DURING ADOPTION        │
        │   (ADULTHOOD)            │
        └──────────────────────────┘
```

```
   ┌──────────────┐        ┌────────────────────┐
   │  FOR SELF    │        │  FOR ADULT CHILD   │
   └──────────────┘        └────────────────────┘
```

• Revising family system
  to single adult, couple or
  smaller household

• Facilitating independence

```
        ┌──────────────────────────┐
        │   DURING ADOPTION        │
        │   (INDEPENDENCE)         │
        └──────────────────────────┘
```

• Accepting mistakes and
  short term re-entries into
  family system

• Developing skills in adult
  relationships

• Forming relationships with
  adoptee's adult partners

```
        ┌──────────────────────────┐
        │   AS GRANDPARENT         │
        └──────────────────────────┘
```

• Coping with reminder of
  own non-biological
  relationship with their child
  or infertility

• Establishing/accepting non-
  biological links with
  grandchildren

Meeting the needs of children who foster

Preparation and assessment

- Children who foster should be fully involved in the preparation for fostering
- Age-appropriate material should be developed for children who foster during the Home Study
- Assessment of prospective foster families should take account of the needs and views of all family members
- Opportunities to meet children who foster should be provided for prospective foster families

Matching

- The needs and views of all family members should be considered when making placements
- When making placements, attention should be given to the key research findings on placement-related factors and outcomes (eg Berridge & Cleaver, 1987)
- Placement agreements should specify the roles and responsibilities of all family members, for example, concerning babysitting, information sharing, etc.

Support

- The right of carers' children to individual support, if required, should be acknowledged
- Carers' children should be offered age-appropriate information and training, to include "safe caring" issues
- Opportunities to meet other children who foster should be made available through support groups, workshops, social events, newsletters, etc.
- Family placement workers should offer support to the children who foster in their link families

Empowerment

- The views of children who foster should be heard and treated seriously
- Representation of the interests of children who foster should be addressed whenever fostering policies or practice are reviewed

Adapted from seminar presentation handout, Gillian Pugh, 1998

Seeking and using support

Background information for social workers

PPIAS

Support from other experienced parents/carers is invaluable for families. **Parent to Parent Information on Adoption Services** now called **Adoption UK**, is a registered charity which aims to provide support, advice and encouragement for prospective and existing adoptive parents and long-term foster carers; membership is also open to agencies. A network of local co-ordinators (who are all experienced adopters) and groups exists in many parts of the country, and Adoption UK also produces an extensive book list, information materials and a quarterly newsletter, *Adoption UK*, now called *Adoption Today*. Further information is obtainable by telephoning: 01327 260295.

Reading for applicants

■ 'Post Adoption Depression', *Adoption UK*, November 1994

■ 'School and the Boy' and 'The Adopted Child at School', *Adoption UK*, May 1995

■ Phillips R and McWilliam E (eds), *After Adoption: Working with adoptive families* Contains chapters on using education services effectively, coping with trauma and attachment difficulties, seeking and using therapeutic help, and anti-discriminatory and anti-racist issues in post-adoption work.

All placements face demands and pressures which at times threaten to overwhelm families' own experience and coping resources, however well developed these may be. An important factor in the success of any permanent placement is therefore the family's acceptance of the appropriateness of seeking help when needed. Such help may be either personal or professional.

The availability of good family support networks is essential and families must be encouraged to develop and access the most appropriate source to meet each particular need. Every family will have its own particular network of extended family, friends, community or religious groups, etc. However, cultural preconceptions and stereotypes about those who will form part of the family's network or can give them the most effective help should be avoided. For example, an Asian family ecomap might have 'God' at its centre.

Caring for children who have had damaging experiences will bring new challenges and it is essential that families can also ask for and use professional support. Professional support should form a lynchpin to every placement; adopters/foster carers, however, also need to be recognised as essentially competent people. This tension must be openly addressed prior to as well as during placement. Families should be reassured from the start that *all* families will need such support at different times in placement and that this is considered "normal" and not in any way a failure by the family. If this is not done, feelings of stigmatisation can deter families from making use of the professional help available. Families also need to know whether there is a choice of service available to them, for example, by being given information about the availability and expertise of voluntary post-adoption centres.

Agencies can make an essential contribution to the healthy survival of placements through providing respite care services as well as both ongoing and emergency guidance and support. Professionals also have a responsibility to signpost other relevant services for families such as therapeutic or educational specialists who may be able to support their work with the child either directly or indirectly. All support services for children,

Further reading for social workers

Phillips R & McWilliam F (eds), *After Adoption: Working with adoptive families* Draws on contributions from social workers, therapists and other professionals, and adoptive parents themselves. Identifies the challenges and problems faced by adoptive families and the range of services they need, highlighting examples of imaginative specialist services which have been established.

'Fostering as seen by carers of children' Part D, in *Adoption & Fostering*, 17 : 2, 1993

Pugh G, 'Seen but not heard? Addressing the needs of children who foster', *Adoption & Fostering,* 20 : 1, 1996

however, need to be carefully tailored to their individual needs and backgrounds if they are to be effective. Obtaining appropriate services for black children or for those with disability, for example, may need more extensive enquiries and additional guidance from specialist staff. Local authority policy and practice should also be able to help by promoting a corporate and interagency responsibility for meeting children's needs through involving other departments such as education, or external services in relation to health and disability needs.

Exercises for applicants

a **USING THE FAMILY NETWORK
FOR SUPPORT**

Ask families to use the diagram they produced
in Module 3, *Contact* (see Module 3, 1b) and to
address the following questions:

- Identify some of the support needs which might
arise after placement.

- Who would you approach about helping you
with these?

b **IDENTIFYING COMMUNITY SUPPORT
AND RESOURCES**

Questions to discuss with families individually or
at a group meeting, asking them to follow up
with further enquires subsequently:

You may need outside help with a child's health
(physical and/or mental), education, disability,
"racial identity", cultural, religious or
language/communication needs.

- What resources do you know of for each of
these?

- What do you need to know more about? (e.g.
the education system may have changed since
you were at school)

- Where might you find out more?

- How might the agency be able to help you?

Learning points about impact, survival and growth

- What have I found out about the support children need within new placements – now? In the future?

....

....

- What have I found out about my own survival needs? My partnership needs (if applicable)? Any existing children's needs (if applicable)?

....

....

- What survival skills would help me? Which ones do I already have?

....

....

- Which do I need to acquire and how might I do this?

....

....

- What areas have I identified that I/we might need support in? How might I use support? What support do I still need to develop?

....

....

- Points of agreement/difference between applicant/s and social worker

....

....

- Areas identified for future development/training.

....

....

....

....

Essential reading for social workers

Fahlberg V, *A Child's Journey through Placement*, Ch.6 Behaviour problems

INTRODUCTION

As we have seen throughout earlier modules, the ways in which parents behave towards their children has an immense impact on the child's development. The interaction between adult and child is at the heart of family life and, as in all close relationships, most will survive many ups and downs over the years while at the same time giving, receiving and being experienced as mutually rewarding.

It is these relationships which adopters and foster carers look forward to most: the opportunity to share their life with a child, to provide a secure and permanent base, and to enable them to grow and develop as a result of the love and care that family life can offer. Yet permanent placement brings with it many potential hazards, and behaviour is a crucial area for applicants to understand in terms of their anticipated role as parent figures and the ways in which many children will express themselves.

This module can only provide a succinct overview of a very complex subject and agencies will need to draw on much additional material in order to consider specific needs. Severe and prolonged behaviour difficulties can be wearing, undermining and destructive of healthy family life. It is vital, therefore, that applicants are given every opportunity to understand and learn about the types of behaviours that are most often associated with children needing permanence. In addition, they also need to reflect on what implications this has for clear, consistent parenting and begin to develop their own thinking and skills in positively managing and changing unhelpful or unacceptable behaviour.

This module will look at some of the most common experiences of children needing permanence, how these may be expressed through behaviour, and consider the impact of positive parenting in effecting change and developing family relationships. While it brings together much of the material within earlier modules such as attachment, identity, expectations, impact, and survival it is not an attempt to provide a resource of strategies and solutions for dealing with problematic behaviour.

Understanding behaviour

■ McNamara J, *Bruised before Birth* Ch.4, 'The challenge of parenting', by Liz Grimes

The ways in which we behave and act towards others are a means of communication, much of which stems from how we see ourselves and our world. We have already seen that our earliest experiences of attachment and intimate bonds are a significant influence on our development. The internal messages we formulate about trust, hope, self-worth, responsibility, reciprocity and confidence will all shape our behaviours and relationships. Our experience of stimulation, learning and achievement enables our cognitive skills to inform our actions and responses. Our social environment will provide us with a variety of patterns and models of behaviour which will impact on our functioning, and our genetic history and personality will also affect how we react and respond to external stimuli.

It may be important to place in context the behavioural needs associated with permanence. To deny that there are additional challenges would be foolish but life, and in particular childhood, is all about working out who we are and how we interact with our world given our particular and unique circumstances. Every child will pass through stages of development that will confront them with new tasks and opportunities for growth and maturation. The parenting role is to acknowledge and understand these common milestones and to support the child throughout these normal but potentially stressful transitions. This will be at the time and pace which are right for them and may well be affected by other needs such as disability, late maturation, etc. So, before considering the additional needs of children placed for permanence, applicants may find it useful to review the normal developmental framework of the childhood years and to reflect on their own experience of learning/teaching behaviour.

a

PARENT MESSAGES (applicants)

Use parent message cards (Fahlberg, 1994, pp370-1) and invite applicants to work in pairs/small groups sharing what messages they received as children and how they think these influenced their behaviour then and now.

- Did their behaviour change depending on circumstances or environment, eg. stressful family times, different ages, at home, school, with friends, etc?

- Why and how?

c

INFLUENCING BEHAVIOUR

- What experience do applicants have of helping children to behave appropriately within/outside the family unit?

- As parents/relatives/friends, what have they observed about what helps/hinders children's behaviour?

- What have they learned about themselves in the process?

Any one or more of these trigger exercises can be helpful either in group, family or individual sessions to promote discussion and debate.

b

PARENTING STYLES

Part 1

Ask applicants to think about the parenting styles they have experienced and to what extent this is/may be reflected in their own parenting.

- For couples/partnerships, what were the differences in the parenting they each received?

- What impact might this have?

- How do/would they avoid mixed messages?

Part 2

Invite applicants to remember a time in their childhood when they did something wrong or naughty, then ask the following. Describe what you did:

- What punishment, if any, did you receive and from whom?

- What did you feel about it at the time?

- What do you feel about it now?

- Would you do the same as a parent or something different? Why?

Making sense of difficult behaviour

Background information for social workers

Info sheet 1   *Understanding how the child became and remains troubled* – Kunstal

Info sheet 2   *Focusing on how the family is affected by the child and how the child can be affected by the family* – Kunstal

Info sheet 3   *Responding to the coded messages of children's behaviour* – Watson

For background material on Protective Factors, see Module 5, *Impact, Survival and Growth*

For synopsis of attachment types/working models, see Module 1, *Attachment*

Reading for applicants

Phillips R and McWilliam E (eds), *After Adoption: Working with adoptive families* Section 2 – 'Adopted children in schools' including three chapters all written by adoptive parents about different educational needs and their impact on placements. Also Section 3 Ch 6, 'Coping with Trauma' and Ch 7, 'Attachment disordered children', both chapters written by adoptive parents.

Van Gulden H and Bartels-Raab L, *Real Parents Real Children*, Section 2, 'Growing Up Adopted: The Developing Child'

Those children requiring alternative permanent families will be dealing with all the normal developmental transitions previously mentioned but these will inevitably be complicated by their individual experience of loss and trauma. Sustained difficult behaviour is a symptom of emotional distress. Behaviour is a means of communication and, when children communicate their pain and confusion in unhelpful ways, the task of the parent is to try to understand the reasons why and to help the child learn new and healthier ways of coping. Applicants may find it helpful to think about behaviour in relation to the following headings. However, it is crucial to note that there are no clearcut divisions as many children will struggle with the combined impact of

all the following factors and more. Their response will often be a complex cocktail of habit, learned behaviour, distorted relationships and emotional pain – it is this challenge which makes positive parenting so important.

Separation and loss

The effect upon the child of separation from his or her family of origin, even for an infant placed for adoption, involves grief. Sadly, the opportunity to grieve, not only for what was but also for what might have been, is not always available to children. The grieving process is important to recall i.e. shock, denial, anger, bargaining, sadness/ despair and resolution. When they are not helped to grieve, children may get developmentally "stuck" in the grief process, for example, in anger, denial or despair, and be unable to move on. Much of their emotional energy is taken up with their pain and loss and there is little left for growth or movement. Children can often close down emotionally and, because their development is "on hold", they can be functioning way below their chronological age in emotional and behavioural terms. It is also important not to focus solely on overt, acting out behaviour as depression is often associated with grieving children although frequently unrecognised. Understanding the implications of appropriate regression and overt teaching/modelling around feelings will be important for applicants to consider.

Similarly, loss will often be a major factor for many applicants and the reality of parenting and/or living with the pain of a hurt child can have a profound impact on parent figures. Social workers will need to prepare applicants for the possibility of a child reactivating their own losses while providing an open supportive relationship which gives permission to grieve without judgement or implied sense of failure.

Attachment

Module 1 considered the importance of attachment and its significance for healthy emotional development. If early attachments have been highly dysfunctional, the child will have very distorted perceptions of adult–child relationships. Primal emotions can be deeply felt and the inner rage that some children carry within them because their early needs were unmet can be both powerful and overwhelming. Within themselves children can feel untrusting and unlovable and wide-ranging aspects of development can be affected such as conscience, learning, self-esteem, initiative, etc (see Module 1). The world is viewed as unsafe and threatening and children seek to re-enact the familiar patterns and models of the past.

Social workers will need to help applicants understand the impact of a poor attachment history and consider how its imprint can affect behaviour and relationships. For some children this will be a long-term undertaking and rejecting, depressed and angry behaviour can, over a period of time, be misconstrued as deliberate and calculated rather than unconsciously motivated. A destructive cycle can then evolve which becomes unbearable for both child and adult(s). The more opportunity applicants have to make sense of behaviour, and the more equipped they feel to manage it, the more likely they will be to find ways of supporting both themselves and the child.

Some applicants may find it helpful at this stage to learn more about the different types of attachment and the damaging internal working models that can result from adverse parenting and insecure attachment. However, this theoretical material will not be helpful to *all* applicants. What is important is that social workers themselves have a good understanding of attachment theory so that they are then able to work alongside applicants in helping them to make sense of specific histories, needs and behaviours and explore the implications for family life. A positive sense of partnership in preparation paves the way for a shared and supportive relationship throughout the placement process.

Trauma

Sadly, more and more children are entering public care with histories of trauma including violence, emotional/racial/physical/sexual abuse and abandonment. Such experiences create enormous conflicts for children which force them to adopt necessary survival strategies. So, for example, because their situation is so unbearable, children may cope by switching off emotionally and not

allowing themselves to experience feelings; their thinking may be compartmentalised in order to shut out the painful areas of their life; and consequently, their world and their identity become fragmented and disorganised. These children often feel fearful and powerless and, because of their learned experience, they view others with suspicion, assigning roles of either victim or perpetrator. Their mindset may be one of extremes; a simplistic approach which does not allow for subtleties or gradations and which sees relationships as being about domination and subordination. Such distorted and damaging perceptions will inevitably touch those who live alongside the child and social workers will need to discuss the ways in which, over time, adults can find themselves in a position of mirroring the child's issues by feeling worthless, powerless, abused, etc. These are potentially devastating reactions and social workers can help applicants to understand and anticipate the power of projection and to think about strategies for managing it.

The impact of early trauma on behaviour will clearly vary according to the child's history, his or her own temperament and personality, the help and understanding available to them in the past, and the degree to which a permanent family can make sense of what the child brings with him/her and work towards helping the child establish different and healthier ways of managing. Applicants will need the opportunity to practise understanding behaviour and to consider the healing aspect of their parenting role. This involves knowing themselves as well as knowing their child. While acknowledging their vulnerabilities they need to be aware of the importance of emotional resilience and support in order to live with the effects of trauma. Holding and absorbing the child's pain and confusion are integral aspects of the healing process but these can be powerful triggers within family life. Parents need to engage positively with their children in order to help them develop increasing self-awareness and a capacity to resolve their own issues as they grow and mature. Anticipating behaviour and understanding its causes can help applicants to feel more confident in proactive parenting, self-care and able to focus more on the solution than the problem.

Exercises for applicants

a

PARENT MESSAGES (child)

Use a case history (see Appendices) and ask applicants to think about the messages that the child has received in the past and what different messages they will need in a permanent family.

Draw out implications arising for different family structures eg. single parents, male/female roles, childless couples, existing children.

Consider issues arising for networks/support systems eg. extended family, friends, religious community, school.

b

BEHAVIOUR, NEEDS AND RESILIENCE

Then ask them to look at the child's behaviours in the light of their history and think about what they might be saying about unmet needs.

- What protective factors can the child draw on? (see Module 5, *Protective Factors*)

- How might these be supported and strengthened?

c

ACCEPTABLE BEHAVIOUR

What would applicants find acceptable/unacceptable behaviour at different ages? Make cards which describe behaviour (see below for some examples) to facilitate discussion about what is/is not acceptable.

- 11-year-old has pornographic pictures

- 4-year-old bites younger sister

- Girl 15 has sex with 19-year-old boyfriend

- 6-year-old kicks and spits at parent in shop

- 13-year-old smokes cannabis

- 8-year-old boy dresses up in girl's clothes

Add your own examples

Understanding how the child became and remains troubled

There are four major areas of "emotional injuries" that need your focus.

1) **Perception** It is very important to understand how the child perceives and misperceives others, especially carers. Think of this as the child's unfortunate and negative "mental blueprint" about self and others. These children often see new carers as a "reincarnation" of the family of the past. Because of this, they attempt to re-enact their painful past family experiences … which can quickly lead to parent-child conflicts arising from their differing perceptions and expectations of family.

2) **Behaviour** Think past the child's behaviour to the meaning behind it. In a sense, you must be a bit of a "psychological detective" with these children. Remember that behaviour is communication. "Bad behaviour" is a distorted and self-destructive way of revealing and expressing needs, feelings, and presses. In essence, 'a child can never not communicate'.

3) **Feelings** Keep in mind that some children don't have the foggiest notion about what a feeling is, and most troubled or challenging children lack adequate ability to recognise, understand, and "give voice" to feelings. Many need a course in "Feelings 101". They must be taught what feelings are, a feelings vocabulary, and how to identify and express feelings. They must also learn to accept negative feelings, and modelling by parents of the acceptability of feelings and how to cope with them really helps.

4) **Relationships** Recognise that many placed children have a poor understanding about how relationships work. They are unaware about how to relate to others in a way beneficial to each. Some emotionally injured children have had an early social education for failure. They to their demise, at times seek to resurrect – through their behaviour, perceptions, and challenges to the family system – the family of the past and in this way undermine the very family they need the most. They must learn mutuality, sharing, and reciprocity with others. There must be a relearning that relationships are more than control, exploitation, or adversity. These children must learn the value of closeness, the security of intimacy, and the fulfilment found through caring.

Taken from workshop material by F. Kunstal, 1998

Focusing on how the family is affected by the child, and how the child can be affected by family

Some brief realities

- When a family takes in an emotionally injured, challenging child … especially if that child is older … they, in a sense, are also "importing the child's pathology".

- Remember that you will be influenced more by these children than they will be by you. These unfortunate but challenging children often have the power and ability to find and exploit your emotional "Achilles heel". At a time when you must parent to your best, these children often succeed in bringing out your parenting at its worst.

- Recognise and be careful to not respond as the "ogre" that these children believe you are, expect and demand to see, and fear that you will be.

- Accept one great parental challenge: To not reject a child who expects, is driven to, and believes in his or her inevitable rejection…and so rejects you. In short, the child launches a "pre-emptive strike".

- Prepare to parent "therapeutically", not just to be caring parents, but to also be healing "agents of change". There is no greater healing power for these children than the care of a good family to undo the destructive remnants of their pasts.

- Have realistic and positive expectations. Rather than survival, demand and expect "thrival".

- Don't forget the needs of the other children/siblings … as unfortunately they can unwittingly become "the forgotten family"; and don't forget your personal needs, and those of your relationship. Your effectiveness in your parenting has much to do with your effectiveness away from your parenting.

Taken from workshop material by F. Kunstal, 1998

Responding to the coded messages of children's behaviour

Behaviour has meaning: people do not act in random and unpredictable ways.

- There is never, however, one single trigger for any act.

- Behaviour is determined by a combination of simultaneous external stimuli and such things as genetic make-up; the body's biochemistry; the expectations of others; learned roles and habits; and by factors about which we are not fully aware because they lie below our level of conscious observation.

In our relationships with other people, however, it is useful to try to identify possible reasons for their behaviour so we can respond more appropriately.

This is especially true for parents as they rear their children.

Some possible reasons that children "misbehave" (that is, behave in ways of which we do not approve):

- Biochemical or neurological triggers over which they have no control

- Learned response from their past which they think will help them manage or control their environment or ward off intimacy which they have learned to mistrust.

- Conscious acts intended to test the limits of their caretakers or teachers.

- Unconscious coded messages of their unmet earlier needs.

Because the needs of many foster and adopted children were not met in earlier years, *their behaviour is frequently a coded message to their parents.*

- Responding to such misbehaviour by punishment, talking things over, or behavioural management techniques is not effective.
  The children may be able to comply and modify their behaviour for a limited time, but the unmet need remains.
  Such responses by adults send the child a message that they cannot read the code and *therefore cannot help the child.*

- The task for the parent is to read the code and attempt to meet the need that the behaviour is expressing.
  The parent must ignore the child's chronological age and ask themselves, "At what age would this behaviour be appropriate?"
  Then they must respond to the child as if he or she were of that age (but always in a way that the child will not find sexually stimulating).

- For instance, the gangly ten-year-old who wants to sit in his mother's lap should be treated as a toddler and allowed to have close physical contact; and the eight-year-old who is having a temper tantrum restrained, hugged, and reassured as one would do for an 18-month-old from whom such behaviour would be expected.

- While the parents must always be clear that they will not tolerate any behaviour that jeopardises the safety of the children or of others, they need to be as generous as possible in the range of responses they accept.

One may think that if a parent acts this way the child will never grow up. To the contrary, *if the parent does not act this way the child can never grow up.*

Taken from workshop material by K Watson, 1998

Positive parenting

The majority of children placed permanently will respond – albeit very slowly at times – to the love, care and commitment of a stable and nurturing family environment. But they will present challenges and the way in which these are understood and dealt with can set the tone for how confident both parents and child will feel. Research has shown that one of the most damaging early influences for children is to grow up in environments of high criticism and low warmth – yet that is exactly the experience of many children who need permanent placements. Redressing this balance and modelling new, more positive ways of relating requires not just an understanding of the behaviour and the healing which is required, but also a clarity and confidence about parenting approaches and continued learning.

Positive discipline will focus on and anticipate good behaviour knowing that children need and value discipline for their own development as well as for the sanity of the adult! Teaching is always an integral part of parenting and many children will need to unlearn well-established but unhelpful patterns and learn different, healthier ways of managing. Becoming trapped in repeated cycles of negative discipline and bad behaviour will only undermine and diminish both child and adult. It will be important for parents to think small and to prioritise the specific areas that seem most important to address at each stage. In this way strategies can be focused, manageable and readily reviewed and monitored.

Parenting a child separated from their family is different from birth parenting. It brings different challenges and rewards and applicants will want to rehearse not only the potential conflicts but also ways of responding and then continuing to adapt. Maintaining responsiveness is not easy in the face of challenging behaviour and applicants can benefit from thinking about strategies that focus on respecting the child, initiating positive interaction, setting appropriate and achievable limits, using attention effectively and modelling care (including self-care), consistency and self control.

Further reading for social workers

■ McNamara J, *Bruised before Birth*, Ch.3 'Roadmaps and decoders', describes ways of helping children exposed to parental substance abuse but many useful and transferable ideas for use with applicants.

■ Phillips R and McWilliam E (eds), *After Adoption: Working with adoptive families* Section V, 'Giving adoptive families a break' and Section VI, 'Therapeutic help'.

Videos

■ *Challenging Behaviour*, BBC

■ *Caring for the sexually abused child,* NFCA

There is a wide range of general parenting material available – see Appendices for further information.

Adoptive and foster parenting is not easy but the rewards can be great and are often underplayed. To see a hurt, confused child slowly begin to heal, trust, achieve, feel good about themselves, take the risk of opening up and even belonging can be one of life's most fulfilling achievements. They have been changed through their experience of family even though sometimes the changes may be very small and take a long time. Social workers need to take care not to be exclusively problem focused! It is vital not to underestimate potential risks and difficulties, but equally vital to recognise strengths and resilience in both child and adult/s. Expectations are key and often applicants will need to be able to take encouragement and hope from small glimpses of progress.

Some of the many materials available about parenting and strategies are listed in the Appendices and include examples of different agencies' experience and practice. While the importance and impact of positive parenting is a critical component of assessment, its relevance increases throughout the placement process. Opportunities for further reflection and learning along with affirmation and peer support need to be continued and expanded post approval and placement.

a

LINKING BEHAVIOUR WITH NEEDS

Part 1

Invite applicants to list different behaviours that they might expect following:

- Early attachment difficulties

- Separation and loss

- Trauma and abuse etc.

Use behaviour 'maps' (see Module 4, Info Sheets 3–5) to aid thinking/discussion.

Part 2

Consider a case history and use the questions below to discuss needs and ideas for strategies that include nurture.

- What has happened to this child? (e.g. abuse, neglect, poor attachments, separation, etc)

- What message has the child received? (e.g. it's all my fault, etc)

- What behaviour do we see?

- What is the child communicating (e.g what meaning are they taking from past events)?

- What messages does the child need to receive?

- How might these messages be communicated?

  a) in structured work with the child on a "coherent story"?

  b) in the care they receive on a daily basis?

- What opportunities can be created to build self-esteem and resilience?

Taken from training material, J Morrison

b

POSITIVE DISCIPLINE

Part 1

Help applicants to consider the impact of different forms of discipline/control on children who have experienced damaged attachments/trauma. Use either the *Discipline Techniques* exercise (see overleaf) to discuss the impact of different discipline on both child and adult and/or the *Discipline and Control* table (Fahlberg, 1994, p286) to promote discussion around assessing needs and considering appropriate responses.

Part 2

Invite applicants to role play situations where behaviour is difficult and rehearse how they would deal with different responses. Use the scenarios set out below, or the case studies in the Appendices or your own experience.

- It's your daughters' 4th birthday – the child you look after/adopted has broken one of her new toys. She is in tears and shouting 'I hate him, I wish he would go away and live somewhere else'. The boy (aged 5) is laughing.

- The bedroom of a 13-year-old girl who has recently been placed with you is dirty and very untidy, she refuses to clean it. This is causing problems with other children in the house who have to tidy their rooms every week.

- Money has gone missing from the place you keep your change in the kitchen. You now keep the money in your purse and it has started to go from there too. You suspect Michelle (aged 8) has taken it, she denies it.

- The boy (aged 10) you look after tells your own children tales of his exciting life before. You know these stories are untrue. His teacher at school has now mentioned that he is making up things about why he lives with you and what his life will be like when he goes back home. He cannot go back home. His own peer group call him a liar.

- A young person (aged 15) has a history of being violent. He asks you for his weekly allowance two days early. You tell him this is not possible and he starts shouting and acting in a threatening manner.

Discipline techniques exercise

TYPE OF DISCIPLINE	WHAT IT TEACHES THE CHILD	EFFECTS ON SELF-ESTEEM	LIMITS ON USING THIS TECHNIQUE	EFFECT ON PARENT
PHYSICAL Smacking				
Washing mouth out with soap				
Holding or restraint				
VERBAL Scolding				
Nagging				
Praising				
WITHHOLDING/ GIVING Not giving food				
Giving extra money for treats				
Threatening to leave				
Withholding clothes				
OTHER Isolation or time out				
Making agreements				
Modelling or showing				
Signalling appropriate behaviour				
Redirecting child's activity Or teaching a new skill				
Grounding				

c

HELPING CHILDREN MANAGE THEIR BEHAVIOUR

Share ideas/suggestions for helping children with their behaviour by using the methods mentioned below and/or case histories (see Appendices) to aid understanding about underlying causes of behaviour and rehearsing different strategies to deal with specific situations.

Use the following methods – or list your own with applicants' help – as a basis for discussion. This exercise could be used with case studies to aid understanding of underlying causes of behaviour (previous material might be referenced e.g. Module 1, *Attachment cycles*; Module 1, *Attachment types/working models,* etc., Module 3, *Components of Self Concept*).

Ask applicants what methods/stratagies might help children placed in effecting positive change in their behaviour? What would not work?

For families with existing children: What works/does not work? Why? How do you adapt?

N.B. Consider the impact of different factors eg. personalities, age, "race", gender, disability, etc.

- Be a role model

- Use time out

- Use positive reinforcement plus privileges

- Withdraw privileges

- Be clear about consequences and follow through action

- Ignore the behaviour

- Getting child to put things right

- Hold family meetings

- Complete behavioural charts

- Use 'house rule'

- Help the child to make sense of their feelings

- Replace negative time with positive time

- Provide alternatives for destructive behaviour

- Draw up a plan for change with the child

- Draw up a plan for change with the child and a professional

Adapted from Child Welfare Institute: 'Group Preparation and Selection', 1992

Using proactive parenting responses to challenging child behaviour

Subtle and profound realities

- Who needs to change first? Parents … their responses, reactions, and approaches to care and parenting. The child's real change will come later, as a "test of time". Although the placement family may not be the source of the child's problems, it is with them – and through "corrective emotional experiences"– that the child can heal.

- Remember: Catching them being good won't work if they are never (or seldom ever) good. Instead, you can help through such efforts as having the child practise "being good", at times reinforcing and providing rewards when the child least expects them, or giving positive and unexpected responses when the child is totally unprepared for kindness. It is important to make love and care unconditional. The child needs your care and closeness the most when he or she feels and behaves least deserving and works to distance you.

- Relatedly, "out-positive the child". You won't help them get "better" if you are always stuck responding on something "badder".

- Using "caring control" and discipline. Keep in mind that the goals of discipline are correction, education and redirection to something better. Discipline to punish may be effective in changing a behaviour in the short-term, but is a worse kind of long-term learning.

- Be careful about which control battles you will enter. Choose wisely. Don't be baited into destructive, chronic conflicts and battles, whose only purposes are to defend against or distance you. If you get into a power struggle, win … especially if the child does not have to lose. Psychologically, be quick on your feet.

- Effective responses to children in a crisis are built when they are not in a crisis. Often, the "little everyday things", such as caring touch, support and sharing, can help the child and family weather later "behavioural storms". Parents must often employ proactive strategies and scripts for change in order to get unstuck, keep the child less defended and off-balance, and alter the course of behaviour problems that are resilient to change and that sabotage the process of the child becoming a healthy family member. The child has to "unlearn" before he or she can "relearn".

- **Use touch sensitively and lovingly ... and a lot. The parent who** sensitively grasps a child also seizes an opportunity.

- Don't underestimate the strength of humour and laughter as powerful bonding tools. One of the greatest losses couples and families experience in caring for a special or extraordinary needs child is a sense of humour. Nothing helps more or quicker in erasing the child's accustomed "life or death" reaction to emotional events. Through humour we are able to bypass defenses and 'speak the unspeakable and approach the unapproachable'.

- Focus on sharing and the "give and take" in family. Try mutual activities, accomplishments, tasks, and rewards to help the child learn that he or she can be a part of family without great personal cost. Caring and sharing also help to 'emotionally refuel' the affectively empty child.

- At times, care for the child according to his or her developmental age. For example, a 12-year-old who behaves in an infantile way, tantrums or "acts like a baby", might very well have younger, unmet needs and hurts that must be attended to before they can "act their age". This can be accomplished through such efforts as "infantalising or re-parenting" for brief daily periods, or simply by activites that tap into the child's early unmet needs (such as holding or rocking the child at times). Some children need to have these early dependency needs met before they are ready to grow. To do this, there also must be a family norm of acceptance, where each child can ask for and receive the developmental caring that is so important to their emotional and relationship healing.

- Keep a balance in responding to the needs of each family member. Don't support or reinforce the other siblings/children for being "low maintenance". And pay as much or more attention to and give as much energy, stimulation, and support for "good behaviour" as you have done for "bad behaviour".

- Maintain and respect the child's connections to early family and the relationships of the past, however weak or tenuous. Our acceptance of and openness to the child's past can help to remove the power it has over the child and preserves remaining connections. Our acceptance of the past also allows the child the experience of understanding and working through losses without self-blame, unresolved anger, destructive longing or idealisation of an absent parent, or self-loathing due to feelings of abandonment or rejection. In these efforts for the child, we want to allow the past to be "a guiding post, rather than a hitching post".

Taken from workshop material, F Kunstal, 1998

Learning points about positive parenting

• **Do you feel you have an understanding of what contributes towards behaviour difficulties for children needing permanence? What have you learned and are there areas you are still unsure about?**

....

....

• **What steps have you taken to prepare as best you can for the impact of certain behaviours on you and your family including extended family/close friends?**

....

....

• **What specific behaviours do you/your family feel more/less confident in dealing with and why?**

....

....

• **In what ways has your thinking changed in relation to dealing with children's problematic behaviour?**

....

....

• **What techniques/strategies have struck you as being most useful in managing behaviour?**

....

....

• **What support/help will you rely on should things get difficult?**

....

....

• **Points of agreement/difference between applicant(s) and social worker**

....

....

• **Areas for further training/development**

....

....

LEARNING PROFILE

Please amend as necessary to suit your agency

1. What specific qualities do you feel you/your family have to offer a child needing permanence?

....

2. In what ways have you changed your ideas about the sort of child you/your family would best be matched with?

....

3. What specific needs/behaviours do you feel best able to handle?

....

    Least able? ....

4. Having reviewed the learning outcomes for each module, list your training/development needs at this stage.

....

    Are there any other issues about which you would welcome further training opportunities?

....

5. What has been most helpful to your learning?

....

    In what ways has your thinking/understanding changed or been reinforced about your role as a parent?

....

6. How would you and your social worker rate your strengths in relation to each of the modules? (two tables: one for applicants, one for workers – 1 is the lowest score and 6 the highest).

* Module	For applicants	For workers
Attachment and Loss	1 2 3 4 5 6	1 2 3 4 5 6
Identity	1 2 3 4 5 6	1 2 3 4 5 6
Contact	1 2 3 4 5 6	1 2 3 4 5 6
Motivation and Expectations	1 2 3 4 5 6	1 2 3 4 5 6
Impact, Survival and Growth	1 2 3 4 5 6	1 2 3 4 5 6
Positive Parenting	1 2 3 4 5 6	1 2 3 4 5 6

7. Having compared your own assessment with that of your social worker, what are the areas of difference? Please note these and agreed plans for moving forward.

....

* Footnote: Include other areas covered in assessment/preparation

Positive Indicators for Successful Foster Carers or Adoptive Parents

1. A special capacity for **empathy** (rather than sympathy) – "to put oneself in the other person's shoes" – to contain the child's projections of "unthought out feelings".

2. The capacity to try to understand the child's behaviour and actions and to make sense of them for the child (an extenuation of Winnicott's idea of "ordinary devoted mothering").

3. Some understanding and previous experience of children and evidence that they have **enjoyed** this.

4. Some evidence that they understand and can manage to contain their **own** emotional (narcissistic) needs (i.e. that the child will not be given this task).

5. If childless, some evidence that he/she/they have accepted this in a way which has not marred their own relationship (i.e. that the child is not needed to repair this "wound").

6. Some evidence that they do not have rigid or "concrete thinking" (i.e. that they can respond to a situation in a "thinking" way, rather than just automatically).

7. Some evidence that they have negotiated **change** well in the past – leaving home, moving house, etc.

8. Some indication that "conflict" has been well managed (i.e. an obvious contradiction would be if a family feud had continued over a long period of time).

9. Some capacity for the parent(s) to accept the child's history, without being haunted by it or feeling their need to use it as the explanation for all the child's future behaviour.

Case Study 1: Marie

Marie is aged seven, a rather solemn looking little girl who tends to look very warily at adults who are new to her.

Both Marie's parents are white, English. They weren't married and her father left home when Marie was a baby. He had occasional contact when Marie was small but hasn't seen her for four years.

Marie's mother, Julie, is a very passive woman who, once left on her own, needed help from her parents. Julie found Marie increasingly difficult to manage once she became a toddler and by the time Marie was four, the nursery school found her very defiant. Julie admitted she found Marie very hard to control. Marie was constantly indulged with sweets and crisps. Julie began to ask her parents more frequently to look after Marie. While this gave Julie a break, and the grandparents said Marie was "fine" with them, Marie started to wet the bed and this became worse as time went on. Eventually Julie took an overdose and was admitted to hospital. At this point she asked for Marie to be placed in a foster home, saying she thought her parents weren't able to care for her "properly".

Julie continued to require treatment for depression after leaving hospital. Marie remained with foster carers who described her as an extremely anxious little girl, constantly checking where they were. She made limited progress at school where the teachers said that she frequently sat in a dream. Julie managed weekly contact with Marie but often had little energy to play with her. Initially contact was also arranged with maternal grandparents but Marie became distressed at this and began to refuse to go.

Marie has now been with her temporary foster carers for two years. A lot of work has been done with Julie during this period to try and help her resume care of Marie and learn how to parent her

more effectively. Julie has spent much of the time talking about herself and is beginning to reveal a very unhappy childhood including sexual abuse within the family. She has now been saying consistently for six months that it would be better for Marie to be adopted.

Marie is now aware of this proposed plan. She says very little to her mother; however, Julie has managed to say to her that although she is sad about it, she feels that it is best for Marie to get a new mummy and daddy. Marie would really like to stay with her foster carers but knows they are temporary carers. Her main concern is that she doesn't want any contact with her grandparents. Julie would like to meet Marie's new family and perhaps have some contact in the future.

Case Study 2: Alex, Kerri and Jason

Alex aged eight, Kerri aged five and Jason aged three are half brothers and sister. All have different fathers – Alex and Jason's fathers are white, Kerri's father is Asian. Few details are known about any of them as the children's mother, Karen, has led a fairly nomadic life on the edges of the drug culture.

Karen is now aged 24. She had spent most of her teenage years in a children's home and was already pregnant when she left care at 16. She resisted any attempts by social workers to offer support to her. She tried returning to her mother but they fell out and she now has no contact with her family. The final straw was the birth of Kerri, Karen's mother couldn't accept a black child in the family. Karen has spent time in hostels, bed and breakfast establishments, with friends and briefly in her own tenancy. She did not stay anywhere long enough for any consistent pattern of care to be established for the children.

Throughout the period that Karen cared for her children, there were concerns expressed by health visitors, social workers, and more recently, teachers and nursery school staff. These included the slow growth of the children and lack of stimulation, for example, leaving them for long periods strapped in the buggy or in a cot. All the children were late in walking and slow in developing speech. On occasions, bruising was noted on the children but there was no clear evidence that this was non-accidental. Alex and Kerri had a few brief periods in foster care when Karen was found homeless and appeared to have taken drugs.

The situation came to a head when Karen brought Kerri, then aged four, to the outpatients department at the local children's hospital with a broken arm. Examination revealed a number of bruises some recent, some older, and x-rays indicated cracked ribs and an old fracture. Child protection procedures were initiated and on

release from hospital Kerri went to foster carers. It proved very difficult to obtain a coherent account from Karen of what was happening in the family. What was clear was that her present partner was very aggressive and refusing to co-operate with anyone in authority. While he usually picked on Kerri when he was in a bad mood, examination of Alex and Jason indicated bruising on them too; they were removed from the family and were placed together in another foster home. At this stage, Alex was very sullen and Jason appeared "frozen". Following this, Karen's partner was charged with abusing the children. He and Karen have split up, but Karen has become very erratic in her contact with the children and now hasn't seen them for over six months. Currently, social workers are unable to find her and an application is being lodged to free them for adoption.

The children are slowly beginning to reveal some of what happened when they were at home, particularly about the level of violence in the household. While much of this was between Karen and her various partners and friends, it seemed that, amongst the children, Kerri was the one most likely to be "in trouble". The three children see each other at regular intervals. Kerri is always keen to see her brothers and likes to give them small gifts she has made. Alex likes to know she is OK but can be very dismissive of her when they meet. Jason's behaviour can be very unpredictable and it is not clear how he views Kerri.

Case Study 3: Jonah

Jonah is an extremely lively noisy six year old. His mother is Jamaican and his father Nigerian. Jonah's father was a student, who returned to Nigeria when Jonah was two, leaving his mother to care for him as a single parent.

Jonah's mum, Lillias, is in her early 30s and met Jonah's father when she was doing a post-graduate course at university. However, over the last few years, she has been unable to maintain herself or Jonah consistently due to recurrent periods of mental ill health. On numerous occasions, she has been admitted to psychiatric hospital after displaying very bizarre behaviour. She will start shouting and screaming for no apparent reason at neighbours with whom she is normally friendly. Her language becomes increasingly florid and she has hallucinations or hears voices but the psychiatric diagnosis isn't clear. Initially, friends helped out with care of Jonah at these times but as they increased, this wasn't possible as a longer-term plan.

After three short spells in foster care with different carers during his mother's hospital admissions, Jonah has now been with the same foster carers for nearly a year. Far from being stabilised, it seems that Lillias' condition is becoming more unpredictable and the possibility has been raised that it may be exacerbated by substance abuse. There are times when Lillias can have very positive contact with Jonah; she plays and talks well to him and they are affectionate. At other times, Lillias' behaviour can be very distressing to Jonah. The foster carers try to protect him from this, for example, screening her phone calls if she rings in a disturbed state. At the same time, they are aware that he becomes anxious if he does not hear from her.

Jonah's carers are an older white couple. They do not see themselves as offering Jonah long-term care. While they find him a responsive little boy in many ways, they are also exhausted by his very demanding behaviour. If anything, they consider Jonah is becoming more confused and uncertain about his future. He talks of wanting to stay where he is or with another white family.

He finds it hard to make friends either at school or around the foster carers home. He is often in trouble at school with other children complaining that he pushes them around or pinches them. However, closer observation in the school playground by the teachers made them wonder if he was being "wound-up" by other children. The foster carer has seen him on various occasions looking very lost when he has tried to join in with other local children and they soon run off and leave him.

Case Study 4: Michael

Michael, aged four, was born very prematurely and spent his early months in the intensive care nursery. There were a number of crises when it was thought he might not survive. While his mother spent as much time as she could manage with him, it was not easy for her as she already had three other children under five at home. Her husband spent long hours working mainly on building sites and was reluctant to take time off because of job uncertainties. Both Michael's parents, Mary and Sean, are from a strong Irish Catholic background but their extended family lived in Ireland and was not available for practical support.

Michael pulled through his various crises but he was a very floppy baby with poor muscle tone and it also became clear that he was blind. Although he went home, his health problems continued and he started having epileptic fits which proved hard to stabilise. It became clear that his development, both physically and mentally, was significantly delayed.

A respite care arrangement was established to help Mary cope with Michael and give her time for the rest of the family. For the first couple of years this worked relatively smoothly although the respite carer began to wonder about the level of stimulation Michael received at home. She felt he probably spent a lot of time sitting in his special chair on the edges of the family.

When Mary became pregnant again, she started to make increased requests for the respite carer to keep Michael for longer periods and more frequently. The respite carer also agreed to foster Michael while Mary was giving birth to her fifth child. By this stage, the respite carer was expressing concern that Michael often had severe nappy rash, he looked pale and lethargic with very sparse hair and had dark rings round his eyes. Mary went into hospital early as there were concerns about her latest pregnancy. The older children were sent to their grandparents in Ireland and Michael was fostered by the respite carer. It later emerged that Mary had, in fact, told her parents that Michael was now in a special home because he needed proper nursing care.

Michael himself settled easily with his carers. By the time he had been with them for three months, he had put on weight, looked much healthier, and was showing far more response to touch and sounds, displaying a particular liking for music. He developed an infectious chuckle. The carers started questioning whether Michael should return to his parents. Mary had telephoned a couple of times to ask about Michael. She had given birth to another boy and was now home. However, she sounded weary, the new baby was a poor feeder and had colic, and she was putting off visiting Michael. She made no mention of plans to have him home.

Case Study 5: Janet and Louise

Janet and Louise are sisters aged nine and three. Their mother, Phyllis, is in her late 30s but looks much older. As a child, Phyllis attended a special school for children with mild to moderate learning difficulties. Since then she has had occasional dishwashing or cleaning jobs but most of the time has been unemployed. Phyllis' first child, also a girl, is now 18 and was brought up by Phyllis' parents. They have no contact. Phyllis left home in her 20s and stayed for a while in a hostel. She began spending much of her time with a group of homeless people and started drinking regularly. It was then she met Danny who is the father of Janet and Louise. He is an older man, now aged 58. He also has grown up children but doesn't see them. Danny had his own tenancy so Phyllis moved in with him and they have now been together for a number of years. Although their relationship is marked by frequent fights, usually when both have been drinking, they are very dependent on each other.

Over the years the family has always been vulnerable and a wide range of supports were offered with mixed success, e.g. family centre placements were valuable, but many days were missed when the parents didn't get up in time to take the children. Many efforts were made to help clean the family home and equip it but standards were very marginal with the children frequently dirty, no adequate clothing available, and concerns about hygiene when the children were small and prone to infections. At the same time Phyllis and Danny were clearly fond of the children. Although the environment wasn't stimulating both parents were physically affectionate to their daughters.

Janet had numerous short stays in foster care when she was small, usually when she was seen by police with her parents when they were incapable through drinking or when neighbours reported her unattended while Phyllis and Danny were at the pub. Each time, after warnings, Phyllis

and Danny vowed they'd do better and things improved for a while but then slipped again.

By the time Louise was born, the family were clearly struggling and foster care was arranged for Janet over the birth. Phyllis and Louise stayed longer than normal in hospital to help Phyllis establish routines, particularly as Louise was a difficult, restless baby. Close supervision was put in place once Louise went home and Janet stayed with foster carers for a further three months before returning home. What became clear was that Phyllis' health was very poor, with her short-term memory severely affected by her alcohol abuse. Danny also was physically less able due to arthritis. The conditions at home deteriorated and both children were finally removed when Louise was just over a year old, after she was burnt when she fell against an unguarded fire while Phyllis was asleep.

They have been in foster care since then. Initially Phyllis and Danny visited regularly but this tailed off. They occasionally contact the social worker to ask how the children are but seem unable to get involved in any coherent discussion about the future.

Janet at nine has mild learning difficulties; currently her reading age is six and she is making slow progress with learning numbers and addition and subtraction. She is a fairly placid girl who rarely questions her situation. However, when she is anxious she bites round her finger nails often until they bleed.

Louise is small for her age, a slightly "odd" looking little girl with some of the features of foetal alcohol syndrome. While she is meeting most of her developmental milestones, her concentration is short. Some of her play is very repetitive while at other times she is all over the place. Louise can be clumsy, and trip over her own feet! When shown photographs of Phyllis and Danny, she doesn't recognise them while Janet now calls them by their first names rather than mum and dad.

Case Study 6: David

David is 10, a little boy with a mischievous grin who is quick to act the clown particularly in front of adults. When new people meet him they are drawn to his sense of humour. He is small for his age, more like a boy of seven or eight.

David's mother, Helen, can be a very articulate person but also very volatile. Her relationship with David's father, Mike, was stormy and twice during the early months of the pregnancy she took the first steps towards abortion but held back at the last minute. By the time David was born she had split up from his father, and still is very angry and bitter towards Mike.

By the time David was 18 months, Helen had established a relationship with Tim who is the father of her two daughters now aged five and two. Tim is very important to Helen although he has assaulted her on many occasions. Right from the beginning, Tim was very involved with David. They had lots of rough and tumble together, went to football matches and were very much boys together. Tim encouraged David to stand up for himself and could not understand the fuss when first of all the nursery school and then primary school expressed concern about David's aggressive behaviour. By the age of seven, David had already been suspended twice from school for fighting and bullying.

When David was eight, Tim was convicted for a serious assault. He pleaded guilty to a reduced charge having originally been charged with attempted murder. He already had various breach of the peace convictions and is presently in prison.

Shortly after Tim went to prison, Helen appeared at the social services offices stating she could not cope with David and stormed off leaving him behind. David went to emergency foster carers while some intensive work was done to try and resolve the situation. Helen proved intractable, she said she had never taken to David, she spoke of him in totally negative terms and said he was only

tolerable when Tim was around. What struck the social worker was the coldness in her manner when talking about David. Helen was much more involved with her dilemmas about Tim, swinging between being angry at him for the way he had treated her and desperately missing him.

Meanwhile, David's emergency carers were seeing more of his aggressive behaviour and, as they also had young children in their care, wanted him moved. He then transferred to experienced foster carers who had older children.

David continues to have very angry outbursts and the school is struggling to cope with him. Helen does not want to see David at all but some contact has been maintained to let David see his sisters, as he very much wants this. David has visited Tim twice in prison; he clearly sees him as his dad and a person he admires.

Appendix III a

Systemic Assessments

The Experience of Barnardo's Family Placement Services, Edinburgh

Sue MacFadyen

Background: why something is different

Undertaking a fostering/adoption assessment is an onerous task. The increasingly complex and sophisticated challenges of fostering/adoption add to the seriousness of the assessment. The wellbeing and future of vulnerable children is at stake. It is understandable that the response to such weightiness has been one of "covering all the angles by gathering a great deal of information", as well as by providing lots of training, Yet, despite the thoroughness and length of some assessments and their Form Fs, something seems missing. The perenniel questions of "what is it that we *need* to know about applicants" and "how best can we find this out" continue to haunt practitioners.

One of the dissatisfactions with traditional assessments, as debated within Barnardo's Family Placement Services, was the fact of most information being content based, which, no matter how detailed, cannot provide a sense of the interaction and dynamic processes between applicants. When a child moves into placement, it is these dynamics and relationships which he/she will experience. For matching purposes at the very least, it seemed important to try and "get at" this area in ways which go far beyond the rather routine information often conveyed under "Family Lifestyle". Drawing on systems theory applications is one way of trying to achieve this (Laycock et al, 1987).

One note of caution: for such complex, multifaceted assessments, no one method or style will suffice. Systemic techniques can complement rather than replace other components of the assessment such as group work, training, in-depth interviews, etc. This diversity of approaches may

be one of the most important safeguards in the assessment.

Working systemically in assessment

- It enables a very dynamic picture of current family functioning relationships, patterns of interaction, rules-to emerge quickly.

- By engaging with the here and now, it provides process evidence – how things work in the family – as well as content material – the facts and figures about the family.

- It involves two workers, one as interviewer, one as consultant who is present throughout the interview. While it is perfectly possible to use a systems approach as a singleton assessment worker, a main benefit of the approach is the co-working, on the principle of "two heads (and perspectives) being better than one", in absorbing and making sense of complex information.

- It can be used expediently at the earliest stages of the assessment to identify applications that should not proceed (Laycock et al, 1987).

- It engages the "whole applicant system" (i.e. the household and/or other key members) in a lively process, avoiding some of the passivity of more traditional assessments. While it is easier to have the whole family present, it is not necessary. The method can be used to good effect with couples and single applicants, especially if "significant others" are invited along, or techniques, such as the empty chair, are used.

- It establishes a focussed way of working with applicants that transfers very effectively to post-placement support.

Systemic practice: the basic principles

The flexibility of systems work makes it ideal for adapting to and fitting around any fixed elements in the assessment. Fundamentally, systemic practice arises from a way of thinking that pays attention to the *connections* between people as well as to each person him/herself. It is these connections which determine and reflect membership of dynamic systems, from family and neighbourhood, through to wider culture and environment, etc. This basic insight is incorporated into traditional Form Fs (now Form F1 and F2) through the widespread use of eco maps. Systemic techniques, which have evolved out of this fundamental principle of connectedness, help to sharpen, refine and focus the information obtained for the assessment.

Another cautionary note is necessary here. The most common application of general systems theory to families is through family therapy. Family therapy continues to evolve through many phases and cycles of new development.

Reimers and Treacher (1995) highlight the pitfalls of paternalism, power blindness and cultural gender determinism that can manifest in strategic family therapies. However, just as family therapy has moved towards more "user friendly" principles, so systemic assessments can also incorporate some of this "second-order thinking" in which the perspective of each individual, as well as the dynamics of the whole, are kept in view by the worker. Similarly, it is possible to utilise the techniques and insights of systemic practice without adopting the classic expert or directive stance associated with some family therapies (Hoffman, 1991). Thus, as well as being probing and serious, systemic assessments can also be collaborative and creative in manner.

What happens in a systemic assessment?

Thankfully there are no rules about this. Systemic practice can be applied in little or large ways, from the occasional circular question, to full scale systemic interviews. Having experimented with different potions within Barnardo's Family Placement Services, the general format tends to be at least two or three family interviews around which are woven other components of an assessment. A further systemic interview as the assessment nears completion is also helpful to check things out, clarify learning and the impact of the assessment on the family.

The main shape and structure of a systemic assessment can be as follows:

(i) Two workers:

- decide between interviewer, directly responsible for engaging with the family and consultant, who observes and records sessions from a slight remove within the room; it is usually preferable to maintain roles within an assessment.

- plan, prepare and debrief before and after each session. Notes from these meetings are helpful in clarifying the themes of the assessment and in preparation for writing the report.

- meet with third worker who acts as systemic consultant to the whole assessment, at least once. This opportunity to process the work and the relationship between the two workers is especially important in difficult or contentious cases.

(ii) Location: office or applicants' home

- Either venue is feasible but with both the space needs to be organised around the demands of the interview, e.g. no interruptions, toys, etc, for the children and a separate room for the break.

(iii) Structure of the interview (guide only)

- Prior to, or as part of the first interview, the methods of work should be explained, permission discussed for any video/screens used, and the overall process outlined. This information can also be incorporated into the Agency letter outlining the purpose, content and timescale of the assessment.

- With the whole family, or members of the household, or single applicant plus significant other, the interviewer leads the session trying to introduce some circularity (see below).

Initial themes might include:

- Whose idea was it to apply and how was that idea shared?

- Why is the application happening now?

- Where is the space – physical – and emotional time for a placement?

• Questions arising from workers' hypothesis (see below) can also provide an entry point into the family system. Keeping sessions time limited is helpful.

• Break: interviewer and consultant leave family (with refreshments!) for 10–15 minutes, to debrief, clarify themes and issues, note points of confusion, etc. and frame further questions and tasks.

• The role of the consultant is crucial here.

• Reconvene to cover issues and questions from the break. This includes the applicants' questions or clarifications, not just the workers'. Agree any tasks or homework to be undertaken for the next session. Close the interview and invite comments on what that was like from the applicants' perspective. With experience and confidence, it is possible to "take the break" in front of the family, thus maximising openness and encouraging greater interaction.

(iv) Follow-up

• debrief and planning

• systematic consultations from third worker

• other assessment tasks shared between two workers

• feedback from training groups and what has been learned can be raised in subsequent interviews

• contentious or challenging areas of the assessment, such as issues of sexuality, sexual awareness and safety, can be easier to open and explore through systemic methods, since the shared focus reduces defensiveness or scapegoating.

Systemic techniques and approaches

Systemic techniques are tools that help us to keep the connections and interactions between members of the system, to the fore. It is this which gives systemic work its very alive, dynamic and present-oriented quality and which, for assessment purposes, helps to give a sharper picture of family rules and relationships than can readily be obtained by linear questions. Tools that can be drawn on include:

• *Hypothesising*

Generating systemic ideas about an application that focuses on conections. The value of an hypotheses, which should arise from the known facts about a family, is not that it must be true or proved to be true, but that it opens up thinking and possibility in relation to what may be around in this family. For example, in a family where the children are grown up and dad has received promotion, two hypotheses might be: 'Mum wants to foster so dad will reduce his work demands' or 'Dad wants to foster so mum will keep busy and not mind his work demands'. These can be explored and discarded, or pursued, through circular questions.

• *Circular questions*

Open questions about beliefs, behaviour and relationships asked of one member about others in the system. In the example above, a circular question might be:

'Dad, what would Mum say are the advantages/disadvantages of your working hours?'. 'Mum, what would Dad notice as the biggest change if you became busier?', etc. For assessment purposes, Burnham (1986, p110) notes that circular questions are a means 'to gather information by asking questions in terms of differences and hence relationships'. Even a few circular questions in an otherwise direct, linear interview will open up information and dynamics and encourage interaction between family members. Children are especially quick at clueing into circular questions. Circularity keeps things fluid and avoids one perspective or storyline dominating and thus closing down other views or options. It encourages curiosity and reflection by members about what happens and how things work within the family system.

• *Neutrality*

An even-handed curiosity on the part of the workers towards the beliefs and behaviours and relationships of each member. Neutrality – perhaps an unhelpful term – describes an attitude of mind or approach that avoids joining or getting sucked into one perspective within a system, something that can all too easily happen in more traditional interviews. Neutrality does not mean being unfeeling or indifferent. Indeed, the workers' awareness of their own emotional response to what is happening in the session is a crucial piece of information. Nor need neutrality lead to misapprehensions or minimisations of responsibility in abusive behaviour (Stratton *et al*, 1990 p.133) Even-handed curiosity helps to avoid defensiveness or rigidity in applicants' responses, thus keeping the process of the interview more open.

• *Reframing*

Paraphrasing from a different perspective along "the cup half full/half empty" lines. This familiar therapeutic technique can be useful in assessments in shifting emphases or in challenging excessively optimistic responses.

• *Practical techniques*

• genograms – used in sessions, provide much historical information and give evidence of communication styles, etc.

• sculpting

• tasks/homework – e.g. each member to bring an object that represents him or her in the family.

Because systemic practice moves away from an emphasis on direct one-to-one talking, it encourages activity and creativity in workers and in applicants, thus providing a greater range of information for the assessment.

Putting it all together

The ever expanding content-based headings of the Form F might seem ill-suited to systemic assessments. In practice, the task of writing up can be less daunting with this method:

• the writing and co-ordinating is shared between two workers

• each planning meeting and systemic consultation is an opportunity to frame headings and organise information for the eventual report. Since the standard Form F headings are for guidance only, they can be amended to reflect the dynamic nature of the

information. For example, "motivation" can be presented as "why this applicant wishes to foster now and where fostering fits into applicant's life"

• the emphasis on present functioning and dynamics can be balanced by historical information being conveyed succinctly through genograms and lifelines. Compiling these with applicants can be an important part of the assessment process.

• feedback from Panels about differently presented Form Fs has been generally positive, with a regular comment being 'the family seemed to come alive more in the report'.

Learning from experience

In a couple of systemic interviews, significant, often deep, areas of relationship and feelings can be opened up. In some cases, this raises the dilemma of the boundary between assessment and therapy. With any type of assessment, applicants will be affected and changed by the process, but the powerful nature of systemic practice highlights this dilemma further. This issue needs to be anticipated and thought through by the agency, particularly regarding agency responsibility when live, painful difficulties emerge in assessment. For example, in a stepfamily who applied to adopt, it became clear after two sessions that the adoption required was that of the youngest child by his stepfather. A third session was used to acknowledge and clarify this, leaving the family with a positive task and a sense of intactness from the experience.

Given the increasingly complex nature of fostering and adoption, it is crucial that an assessment provides both a dynamic picture of current processes and relationships and a deeper investigation into attachment patterns and expectations arising from applicants' own experiences of being parented. These two areas are of course interdependent. For example, clarity about the nature of the marital relationship gained from systemic sessions can be used to explore in more depth and individually, the primary attachment experiences of each partner.

Finally, as fostering and adoption become more challenging, so there is a growing need for carers to bring a reflective awareness to themselves and their responses to the child. Identifying and developing this reflective capacity are an essential part of assessment and training. A systemic approach, by its very style, encourages applicants to pay more attention to their reflections about themselves and others in their family so that their reflective capacity is both clarified and nurtured and developed. One of the most frequent comments from applicants after a systemic assessment (which is usually accepted as readily as we expect applicants to accept traditional methods) is that 'it made us think about things in ways we hadn't done before'.

The IAS Preparation and Assessment of Families

Ruth Watson and Mary James,
Independent Adoption Service

At the Independent Adoption Service (IAS) we have developed an assessment preparation process which begins with two intensive workshops and a team interview focussing upon the needs of children and the adoptive task after which applicants are seen on an individual basis to complete the home study report. The approach draws upon systemic family therapy techniques and aims to help families be better prepared for the task of adoptive parenting and the adjustments which are needed.

The aim of the IAS preparation and assessment of families is two fold. Firstly, to educate families about the needs of children from the care system and the task they could be taking on in caring for such children. Secondly, to make an assessment of their ability to cope with that task. Our process also aims to allow them to play an active part in their own assessment and in the assessment of other members of the group. We are aware that most of the children placed will be of school age and a large number will have been sexually or physically abused. All the children will carry their own "luggage" from the past.

For their part the families often come with the pain of not being able to have their own child, and an important element of their moving on to being adopters is the realisation that adoption cannot give them the child that they would have had themselves. Many of the applicants may have seen a child featured in a newspaper, heard about the agency from others, or indeed looked us up in the Yellow Pages.

Following an initial enquiry, all potential adopters are invited to an Information Meeting, which tells them about the children needing families, IAS and how we work. If after this they complete and return an application form, they are allocated a social worker who offers two preliminary interviews. At these initial meetings, applicants may be screened out either by their worker or they may decide themselves not to go ahead. Interviews also give an opportunity for the applicants to raise personal issues – perhaps a particular health problem, an anxiety about a second marriage, a past criminal conviction or any others.

Before an application commences, all necessary medical reports, references, legal documentation of residence, marriage, police, social services, accommodation and safety checks are carried out.

The social worker who sees the family at this preliminary stage will be their worker throughout the process. The aim is that the worker will form a relationship with the applicants, which will be based on shared knowledge and a mutual trust. Potential adopters may feel uncertain about the step they are contemplating, about what is to be expected of them and what they envisage the evaluation process will be. Hartman describes this type of interview as undertaking the task of reaching a common understanding, clarifying roles, identifying shared goals and specifying the steps to be taken to reach these goals. This is the process of engagement and the beginning of making a contract and a relationship.

The applicants are then invited to two workshops. The workshops have two aims, educative – in which the group members learn about adoption, and assessment – in which we share our expectations of them as potential parents. The aim is that the group will provide an educational experience which will also help a self-selection process so that potential adoptive parents who choose to continue with their application will achieve a good understanding of what may lie ahead. The group members will contribute from their own experience and learn from each other. These groups do not set out to be in any way therapeutic although in practice there may be elements of this.

The co-ordinators do not make interpretations nor are group members pressed to look at feelings. On the contrary, the group is highly structured and directive; however, we do feel it is important that infertile couples share their experiences and so gain mutual support. It has been noted that the experience of being able to participate in their own assessment can be helpful in itself.

The workshops are held on two consecutive weeks. Normally there are two co-ordinators. At IAS, we always aim to have black and white co-workers. Sometimes a student social worker will also participate. The size of the group varies between four and eight families. These may be single household adopters or couples. The groups will be mixed in terms of the applicants' background and racial origins. The techniques we use within the workshops have been developed in systemic family therapy practices.

From a family therapy system perspective, the family is viewed as an open system immersed in their environment. The techniques used in the group attempt to capture the complex dynamics of the family system and are designed to explore the ways in which a family functions, how its members communicate with one another, its composition and hierarchical structure, and its rules and boundaries. Appropriate consideration is also given to the systemic evaluation of each family in relation to its wider network comprising the extended family group, the community in which the family lives, and others involved including professional agencies.

We begin the workshop with an introductory exercise. Each couple is asked to pair with someone who is not their partner and if there are single persons they form a threesome or work with another member. Ideally, we always like to have more than one single parent in each group. We ask all group members to discuss their hopes and expectations and to feedback what they have learnt about each other. This exercise ensures that from the outset everyone participates.

This is followed by a similar structured exercise, this time in same sex pairs, discussing the impact of infertility on them and their lives. This is a difficult exercise but it is very important. If the infertility issue is not addressed early in the workshop then

sometimes it can hang over the proceedings and prevent progress.

Next, we focus on how parents can bring up children to be part of a multiracial society. This is done as an individual exercise each participant writing down four things they feel thy can do to help to achieve this and one thing which may get in the way of the aim. This is an important exercise for all our families. Families then share their thoughts, which lead on to a general discussion and role-plays focussing on some of the issues raised.

Time is spent next looking at where children needing families come from and how they are affected by the loss of their own families and the experiences of being in the care system. We focus on the fact that a child cannot leave one family and join another without everyone being affected. In order to do this we use the technique of mini sculpting. Everyone is given a role in the sculpt. They act out silently and under direction the removal of a child from their birth family and their introduction into an adoptive family. The child is introduced to the adoptive family for several weekend visits. This is done by moving the "child" in and out of the "adoptive family" until the family has reorganised itself. Sometimes the families are torn apart by the child and sometimes they are able to organise themselves more comfortably depending on the particular group. To facilitate this, the child is taken out and given instructions to present the family with difficult behaviour. All of this is done non-verbally except for varying points during the sculpt where members in role are asked to give feedback about how they felt in the positions they held, what they could see, and what their bodies told them.

This exercise is most useful. It helps the group look at the child in his or her original situation and gives some insight into the impact adoption may have on the child, the birth family and the adoptive family. The sculpt exercise has the power of simplicity which can be helpful to highlight the closeness and distance in family relationships, allowing applicants to see in a concrete way how they may need to reorganise themselves to make space for an adopted child. Also, it illustrates clearly how when any one member changes position in the family, change will also occur for the rest. We build on this to begin to consider where children come from and the events which may have taken place in their lives resulting in their being taken into care. The importance of contact between siblings and other members of the family is also addressed in this exercise.

In the preliminary interview, the family will have been shown how to make a family map going back to and including grandparents. These maps are presented in the workshop and commented upon in relation to adoption issues. The purpose of constructing the family map is to help participants see themselves in the wider context, think about their family support system, and consider their family's attitudes towards their proposed adoption. In family therapy, the family is seen as a transactional system, which hopefully is in constant interchange with its extended environment and developing intergenerationally through time. This is a most helpful concept to see in adoption

The family map gives information about the applicants in terms of social and emotional history, and includes dates of birth, marriages, divorces, re-marriages and deaths, lines of closeness and distance, and the capacity for growth and change. It may also help potential adopters understand the implications of their interest in adoption and the possible outcomes of altering their family system by the addition of a new member. At its very least, the family map is a useful way of gathering and organising family history.

At the preliminary interview, the families are asked to construct their own support system. Whilst the primary aim of an Eco map is as an assessment tool, it is also a visual aid around which to integrate the details of the adoptive family's relationship with the outside world. It helps adopters to look at the support and stresses within their wider social network. The Eco map is constructed by writing the family members' names in a circle in the centre of a sheet of paper and then writing about relevant facilities, resources, recreational activities, friends, finance, house, garden, etc, in circles around the family. The family then indicates the nature of their connection to

these resources by drawing lines to represent positive strengths, stress and indifference. The information that emerges from this work may range from a simple assessment of the resources available to an indication that more work on the support system will be required. This exercise helps potential adopters begin to consider whether they will have sufficient support and resources nearby if a child is placed. They are also helped by feedback from the group on how they see strengths and areas where work may be needed.

At the end of the first day, families are given a scenario of a child from the care system in the age range which they have expressed an interest and asked to make a life story book to bring to the next workshop. To help them with this task, they receive information on making life story books. They are encouraged to make the books colourful, ethnically and culturally relevant, and child centred, but at the same time to address the painful and difficult issues of the child's background. Prior to beginning this task, we do a memory exercise whereby each participant is asked to write down an important memory. The worker then collects these memories and throws them away. This is a powerful way to begin discussions about why it is important to help a child deal with past experiences no matter how difficult. In the final session of the day, each person gives feedback on one thing they thought was helpful and one that was not.

The second day begins with each member being given an opportunity to reflect on what they have or have not gained so far. We then move into an exercise in which each member takes a written statement and indicates if they agree with this. Other members of the group comment in turn on the same statement. These statements are quite provocative with the aim that people start thinking about where they stand on difficult issues some of which they may not have previously addressed. The statements are varied with some of a sexual nature e.g. is it ok for parents to walk around naked in front of a child; or are homosexuals more promiscuous than heterosexuals; or is it ok for a girl of 9 and a boy of 11 to share a bedroom?.

Important issues to be addressed in adoption centre on separation and loss. We begin to explore these by asking each person to share a personal experience. Some may be quite trivial but others may be significant. This is a powerful exercise and frequently the pain of the memories is very evident. The co-ordinators acknowledge these feelings and then use them in order to focus on the pain of the children, what they may bring with them to a new family, and how this may affect their relationships and their behaviour.

This leads into applicants beginning to think about the sort of behaviours they would be good at handling or would find difficult. Work is done on this as a series of role-plays. A member of the staff team plays the role of the child with each couple acting as parents. Following each role-play, group members who have not participated in the role-play are asked to comment about how they might have envisaged themselves dealing with similar circumstances. The purpose of the role-play is to help potential adopters think about themselves as parents dealing with difficult behaviour and begin to focus on some of the issues in parenting children of various ages. It also engages the group in looking at the issue of discipline. This is followed by the group giving their responses and discussing various methods of discipline.

Some time is spent looking at the issue of contact between the adopted child and siblings as well as other birth family members including grandparents and birth parents. The fact that, at the very minimum, adopters will be expected to provide a letter and photograph on an annual basis and increasingly there may also be some direct contact between themselves, the child and people from the past is highlighted. Time is spent discussing the fears and anxieties which are engendered by contact.

The importance of openness in achieving healthy adoptions is addressed in the groups and throughout the application process. Applicants need to be able to cope with the past no matter what it contains so that they can deal with this in a way to help the child to understand and accept the past and live with its truth. The life story book which applicants have prepared is used in a role-play with applicants in the role of parents reading it to a child. Preparing the book, and using it in

this way helps to highlight the difficulty that many families have when putting in writing and words some of the child's painful experiences. Sometimes applicants may need to go away and make another book, but in any case, it is a way of practising and rehearsing for the future.

In one of the final exercises, each family is invited to indicate their areas of strength and the areas on which they need to work. Other members of the workshop are also invited to comment in a similar way. This participatory assessment can be most helpful and applicants sometimes hear messages from other members of the group more clearly than they would from the social workers.

In the closing exercise of the workshop, each applicant is asked to comment on one thing they have gained from the workshop and one thing they would have liked.

After each workshop, the staff team meets to debrief and consider the key issues which emerged for each applicant. The applicants' responses and performances in the various exercises are recorded for their individual case records.

Following the workshops, applicants are invited to attend a team Interview. This involves an interview by one member of the workshop team whilst the remainder supervise from another room. This is facilitated by the use of a video, the interviewer being contacted by the team if they wish to ask questions or focus the interviewer in a specific direction. Basic information about the couple already gathered is used to find out more about them as a family system and to explore any issue about which concerns may have been felt. The team interview uses the systemic family therapy approach to interviewing based upon hypothesising, circulatory questions and neutrality to engage couples in their assessment and learning process.

The team at IAS has modified these principles, in particular the use of circular questions, to engage couples in their assessment. The belief is that our perceptions of others' behaviour and others' perceptions of our own behaviour provide feedback loops, which make possible important emotional attachments. As the family develops, each member continually gives and receives feedback about his, her and others' behaviour and this mutual feedback modifies the family units' range of interactions towards predictability and a stable pattern. However, the family system is also constantly interacting with the elements of other systems, including various stages of biological development of communities, schools, etc. The relationships within the family are thus constantly in flux. Therefore, there is a basic paradox that we depend on close stable patterns in relationships to give us feedback, yet these important relationships are always changing because of biological development and external influences. Some families seem well able to cope with this dilemma by being focused enough to reorganise their interactional patterns and others are more uncertain about change. The purpose of exploring family organisation in this context is to find out its degree of flexibility.

In thinking with the family about adoption, it is important to consider the nature of its rules. One of the most important issues revolves around the family's adaptive style. Is it flexible enough to provide room for individual differences and change while remaining sufficiently the same to provide coherence, stability and continuity? These issues are important for all families but of special significance for families considering adding a child from the care system to their home.

Another consideration to explore during the team Interview is family boundaries, that is to say, the invisible line that separates what is inside the family and what is outside the family. It is important to assess how open and flexible the boundary around a family system is because it is likely that this will be tested by a new person coming to the home with different values, behaviours and attitudes.

The nature of the boundary around the family has considerable relevance for decision making around adoption. If a family has a relatively close boundary and tends not to allow outsiders to become part of the family, adopting a child, particularly an older one, could be painful and difficult as they may never allow the child to belong. At the other extreme are families who tend to be completely open yet may not be able to offer the continuity, stability and sense of

belonging that a child needs. Such families are also unlikely to have the support network required for taking on such a demanding task.

As a starting point for the team interview, we form an initial focal hypothesis from the information we have gathered from the group about the applicant's interaction as to what role the child would play in their family system and in which areas they may have difficulty in accommodating a child. The interviewer aims to take a neutral stance in order to look at family interactions and is greatly assisted in doing this by having the immediate support of the team.

Towards the end of the interview, the interviewer withdraws for consultation with the team and then re-enters to positively frame the contributions the couple have made during the session. The team may be happy that the applicants proceeds to the next stage of the process or suggest that the interviewer ask them to continue to work on a particular area of concern within an agreed time scale.

The final stage of the application process is the home study. This takes the form of individual meetings with the applicants in their own home and at the office. During these interviews, any issue identified from the workshop as needing further work will be addressed. The applicants' individual personal history, personal relationships and life style are explored and identified so that the full home study report for presentation to panel can be produce. All applicants see the completed home studies and contribute to these as they wish.

The Road to Placement

Jane Horne

Barnardo's New Families, Colchester

Introduction

What are we seeking to achieve when we set off down the road to placement with prospective adopters and foster carers? Do we look beyond approval when constructing programmes for preparation and training? Are we overplaying the role of assessment in protecting placements? Are we under-resourcing the other ingredients that go towards making and maintaining a stable placement? Does our assessment process help applicants make the decisions they need to make, or are they more concerned with helping us make ours?

These were just some of the questions we were seeking to address in reviewing our work. The outcome – a model that introduces task descriptions – is explicit about the criteria used to evaluate new applications and seeks to produce evidence based assessments.

> *As a prospective adoptive parent you haven't got many cards to play. You have to get the social workers to like you. We turned our conversations with them around to the difficulties of their jobs and the hassles and office politics in their departments. Our meetings turned into empathy building exercises. We didn't really ask them for anything, so they couldn't refuse. We didn't go on about our failed attempts at fertility treatment, show them an empty nursery and say how much we longed for children. Give them lots of tea, nice biscuits and, above all be a good listener – they love it.*
>
> Extract from article in
> national newspaper, Jan 1999

I hope this couple who were involved in an assessment some 10 years ago were

underestimating the work done by their social workers in preparing them for the eventual placement of the children they adopted. However, what they have to say about the powerlessness of their situation and the lack of control they experienced as adults who in other parts of their lives held responsibility is important.

The New Families Project

The New Families Project is part of Barnardo's as an adoption agency. The Project has 20 years of experience of placing older children in permanent substitute families. The Project also operates a Bridge Fostering scheme offering short contract-based placements with fee paid foster carers. We have a team of post adoption workers offering a range of services to children, their substitute families and birth families. The majority of the children referred to the Project for placement have histories of abuse, multiple moves, poor attachments and resulting challenging behaviour. Supporting ongoing contact is a regular feature of our work.

Over the past 20 years the New Families Project has developed in response to many changing factors including a greater understanding of the impact of trauma, abuse, separation and loss. We have sought to address the issues raised by ongoing contact; new legislation; concerns about quality; and importantly, issues raised by those who have been adopted, their adoptive families and their birth families.

Decision making

In recent years the Project has begun to focus on the nature of decision making in agencies like our own and the impact of this on children and adults using our services. It seems self evident to state that processes are in place to enable the agency's decision making. It is, however, an important point to take on board when looking at whether we do enable partnership with applicants or empower them for the challenges ahead. It is essential for agencies to have procedures in place that help them to make decisions. Practicality and regulations require this. It is equally important to recognise that, in matters such as adoption and fostering, the agencies are not the only ones who have decisions to make.

Practitioners and managers comment on the issues raised in involving children in meetings or applicants in Panels. Perhaps it is precisely because these meetings are not designed to facilitate the decision making of children or of applicants but of the agency, that these issues arise. Agency systems of decision making often take little account of the fact that the central characters in any "case" have decisions of their own that they are making alongside those being made by the agency. If we are truly seeking to work in partnership with applicants seeking to adopt or foster (or with anyone else), we do need to ask ourselves whether we know the criteria they are using to make their decisions and whether we know the criteria we are using.

Objectivity and criteria in decision making

That there is no true objectivity is a concept I hope most of us would accept. However, criteria are used in any decisions on establishing an applicant's suitability to adopt or foster. It is one thing to question whether it is possible to establish firm criteria but it is another to avoid tackling the fact that they are being used.

A recommendation (or not) to approve an application is a life changing decision. It does seem important to know that these decisions are being made on the basis of some shared understanding at the very least between social workers and Panel members, as to what qualifications, experience, knowledge, skills, and abilities best equip an individual to adopt or foster in the late 1990s.

When we began to review our approach to the preparation and training of prospective adoptive parents and foster carers, we were asking ourselves a number of questions, none of which were particularly new to us or in the field (Ryburn, 1991).

- What criteria are we using to evaluate an applicant's suitability to adopt or foster?

- As no decision can be made without criteria being in play, are these explicit?

- Without explicit criteria how could we be sure that no discriminatory or oppressive practice was in play in the recommendations made to Panel?

- How did we know that the training that we offered did indeed address the development of the abilities and skills applicants would need?

- How could prospective adopters and foster carers make the decisions they needed to make about their own suitability without the knowledge of what the task entailed?

- How could applicants evaluate their experience, skills and abilities and identify any gaps which they needed to work on, if they did not know what would help or undermine their bid not only to be approved to adopt or foster, but also to do the task with some sense of gain for themselves and the children?

The Adoption Agency Regulations and the Children Act Guidance and Regulations – Family Placements (Vol 3) together with the guidance for BAAF Form F all indicate the information to be included in a report to Panel. In part they tell us why this information is useful in evaluating suitability but the basis for interpretation of the information is not made explicit (Trisiliotis, Sellick and Short, 1995).

The road to placement

As part of the review of our practice we developed the analogy, already used in training, of the "road to placement". The more we worked with this analogy the better able we were to see the whole road from the applicant's point of view and to take on board fully, what in fact we already knew, that for applicants the ultimate destination is not approval but placement and beyond.

Feedback from approved adopters and foster carers indicated that they saw the "vehicle" we used in preparation as "comfortable" and "well maintained". They also viewed the worker as invariably a "good driver" but they did not always know where they "were going until they got there" nor "how long the journey would take". We appeared to be giving a good lead along a road we knew well and which was unfamiliar to applicants. However, the applicants were in danger of feeling out of control, having no "map" of where they were and why, and no clear view of the road ahead.

In addition, we were able to see that the "vehicle" used on this part of the road was quite different from that used when looking at a link and different again to that used at placement. At placement we could "see" applicants getting into a "vehicle" owned primarily by them but which was new to them (parenting through adoption/fostering). We began to ask ourselves in what ways our approach on assessment and training had prepared them for these crucial stages "on the road".

Historically, agencies like our own have been in existence to take applicants to Panel and make placements. It is only in recent years that we have begun to grapple with the needs of children and families post placement/adoption. Has the part we have so long played telescoped our view on to one end of the "placement road" i.e. the beginning, where we can offer intensive support and assistance? Has the result been that we have not given as much emphasis as perhaps we should have to the need for applicants to maintain control over themselves in the process, and learn to develop their confidence to work independently.

Conclusions of the review

After a period of debate and consultation, the group leading the review reached a set of conclusions which shaped the development of the new model.

- The purpose of the preparation and training is to prepare applicants for placement of a child traumatised by abuse.

- In the process of achieving this purpose, applicants and staff evaluate the applicants' suitability and a report is written for the Child Placement Panel (Adoption and Fostering Panel).

- Applicants need to feel an increased sense of control over themselves as participants in their preparation and evaluation if they are to feel in control when a link is being planned and on placement of a child.

- Applicants, as well as the agency, need to feel they have space to make their own decisions on the appropriateness of proceeding with their application.

- If applicants are to be able to evaluate their own suitability they need to understand the task; and to have access to the qualifications, experience, skills and abilities assumed important in undertaking the task.

Task description

The task description is one of the "maps" we now give to applicants to help them decide whether the road to adoption or fostering is one they wish to travel.

It developed out of our realisation that whilst we had many packs of information, reading lists, etc, we had nothing in place to give to those applying to adopt or foster through our Project that succinctly described the task they would be expected to undertake if they were approved as adoptive parents or foster carers.

As workers we agreed that if we were looking for employment we would expect to receive something in writing which outlined the task we would be doing if we were successful in applying for the job. Indeed the task description would influence whether we applied in the first place. Was it not reasonable to afford adoptive parents and foster carers the same opportunity?

A task description and person profile for adoption had been written some time before and we went on to construct such descriptions for all the different tasks applicants could undertake with the Project including bridge fostering, long-term fostering, and short break care.

We recognise that adoptive parents and foster carers offering permanent substitute family placements to children do not see themselves as applying for employment. We also recognise the differences in motivation between adoptive parents and foster carers. However, some children placed directly for adoption or permanent fostering by the Project could as easily have been referred to the Bridge Scheme. Whether someone is seeking to provide a short-term care service for "looked after" children or to develop a personal relationship with a child as a lifelong parent, the issues the children bring and the task to be undertaken can be just as challenging. We concluded that prospective adopters need the same clarity about tasks as Bridge Carers.

Reproduced at the end is the task description for adoptive parents. Now that the task as we frame it has been written down, we can more readily discuss it with new applicants, with approved and experienced carers, and with young people, and thereby review and refine it as a working tool.

Person profile

The Person Profile is another of the "maps" we now give to applicants. Once we focussed on what we were looking for within the information we collated for Form F Reports, we were able to put together a person profile.

In employment any one seeking a job expects to receive a person profile as an indicator of what qualifications, experience, skills and abilities the employer believes will enable the individual to do the job. This helps the job applicant in several ways. Firstly, it gives the applicant information on what the employer sees as being essential or desirable qualifications, etc, to undertake the task. It gives the applicants an opportunity to measure their qualifications against those listed and make some appraisal of whether this is a job for them. It also helps the applicant to prepare for interview.

Increasingly, at interview employers use exercises to draw out evidence of an individual's qualifications and abilities. Employers also recognise that they need to provide induction and in-service training to help the job applicant develop their abilities to do the job. New social workers in Barnardo's undergo a period of

probation at the end of which they are appraised as to whether they can do the job.

This process of interview, induction, in-service training and appraisal has many similarities with the process of preparation, training and assessment followed by those seeking to adopt and foster. Why, therefore, should they not have a person profile made available to them?

We know that those seeking to adopt and foster do not come forward as blank canvasses. They bring with them life experience, skills and abilities that need to be recognised and valued. Being encouraged to identify these from the outset can empower applicants by underlining what they do know already and can enable them to be open about the gaps in their skills and experience.

We know from our own experience and from work on disruption (Fitzgerald, 1983; Smith, 1994) something of the factors that contribute to the stability of a placement or undermine that stability. The person profile seeks to build on this knowledge.

As an agency we have an explicit value system which directs and influences all our work. In addition, whilst we are eclectic in the approaches we use to work with and support children and families, we know that at any one time we will tend towards some approaches over others in child care. We aim to share the core basis of our approach with applicants. We ask them to decide whether the philosophies and approaches underpinning our work are ones they feel they can subscribe to. We make no claims that these are the right or only ways to view issues or tackle difficulties.

Reproduced at the end is a person profile for an adoptive parent. Now that we have made an attempt to be explicit about the criteria on which we evaluate an individual's suitability, the relevance of these criteria can be debated. They can also be reviewed and redrawn in the light of this debate and new research.

Evaluating suitability

The Project acknowledges to applicants from the outset that final decisions about an application will be made by Barnardo's nominated decision maker and/or a local authority on the basis of the recommendation made to the Panel and of the Panel to the agency. Applicants attend the Panel discussion of their application and any subsequent link (Trent, 1990) (Horne & Haunton, 1994).

This is not a system of self-assessment as such. The task for applicants and their individual social worker is to prepare a report which details evidence of the qualifications, experience, skills and abilities on the person profile. The worker will seek corroboration of information and evidence presented by applicants both from their own observations and from friends, family, referees and professionals who know the applicants.

Fully conscious of the brief to protect children, the Project has sought within this system of preparation and training to take on board the messages from work on the behaviour of potential abusers and paedophiles, and has developed a guide for staff designed to enable a risk assessment (Overett, 1998).

Prospective adoptive and foster carers who are clear about their own skills and abilities are much more likely to be able to sift through the information they receive about a child when planning a link and evaluate whether they can offer what the individual child needs.

Conclusion

At New Families, as in most agencies, we want applicants, in whom we invest resources, to succeed in their applications to adopt and foster. We have made an attempt to be explicit about the criteria we use both within the Project and for applicants. We feel this will enable us to be more confident that the decisions we and applicants are making are rooted in some appreciation of the task ahead, an understanding of what can protect or undermine stability in placements, and which are freer from individual prejudice.

As agencies we are engaged in finding family placements for a range of children of different ages and needs. There may not be a common task description or person profile agencies can use although some elements may be the same. Any agency looking at using either of these tools will need to identify the task their carers are being asked to undertake and consider the qualifications, experience, skills and abilities that will assist them in this task.

By using the task descriptions and person profiles we believe we will be giving applicants more information with which to self evaluate. We will also be better able to acknowledge what they bring with them to the task and to identify, with them, the areas in which they may need extra support. We will be affording them more control over themselves in the process of preparation whilst fulfilling our responsibility to structure the preparation and training process. We believe we will also be on more solid ground in appraising their suitability to undertake the task on the basis of evidence of appropriate qualifications, experience, knowledge, skills and abilities.

Full information on all aspects of the model will be available in summer 1999.

TASK DESCRIPTION – ADOPTIVE PARENT

The task description has been designed to give you a feel for the demands made of adoptive parents. Some of course are the same as those made of any parent. Some are different and come with parenting a child who was not born to you, who is "looked after" by a local authority and who has spent part of their life with other people who will be significant to them in different ways.

Purpose of adoption

- Assumption of full parental responsibility for a child making a commitment for life.

- Assumption of all legal obligations of the role of parent to a child.

- Assumption of responsibility for the health and welfare of a child.

- Assumption of responsibility for ensuring a child understands their history and origins.

Major tasks

- Child's origins and history.

- Child's physical development.

- Child's emotional development.

- Child's education.

- Child's social contacts.

- Child and family's support network.

Origins and history

Values a child's history and the importance of people from the past.
Promotes a balanced view of the past for a child.
Acknowledges the difficulties in a child's past without judgement.
Actively looks through and discusses a child's life story material with them.
Encourages positive contact with people from the past now and in the future.
Lives with difference.

Physical development

Understands the needs of children.
Provides adequately for the physical needs of a child.
Does not use physical punishment to discipline a child.

Emotional development

Understands the needs of children who have been "looked after".
Encourages a child to feel good about themselves.
Sees a child as an individual with a past that did not include them.
Values a child as she/he is.
Promotes a strong sense of personal identity in a child.
Spends time with a child one to one.
Sees the world through a child's eyes and responds appropriately.
Offers attachment.
Promotes trust.
Is consistent in approach.

Education

Close liaison with the school.
Visits the school.
Takes an active interest in a child's school/home work.
Encourages a child to value learning.
Supports a child's attendance at school.

Social contacts

Works with a child on making and keeping friends.
Encourages a child to bring friends home.
Takes a child to social events involving friends.
Encourages a child in joining groups/clubs.
Maintains links between a child and other adopted children.

Support network

Establishes support systems for a child and other family members.
Advocates for services for a child and the family.
Works in partnership with the adoption agency.
Asks for the support and advice of the adoption agency.
Asks for and capitalises on the support and advice of professional staff.
Identifies and uses supports before pressures become unmanageable.
Looks constructively at problems and at options to solve them.
Takes advantage of training opportunities through the adoption agency.

PERSON PROFILE – ADOPTIVE PARENT

This essentially is a list of those qualifications, experiences, skills and abilities which we identify as essential in an adoptive parent if you are to be able to undertake adoption of an older child through the Project which results in an emotionally satisfying experience for you and the child alike.

We will base our evaluation of your suitability to adopt through the Project on the evidence you can share with us that demonstrates that you have these qualifications, these experiences and these abilities.

Basis and values

Actively promotes the philosophies underpinning Barnardo's Basis and Values.
Shows an awareness of issues of race and discrimination.
Actively promotes equality of opportunity.
Has a strong sense of personal identity.
Is tolerant of difference.

Qualifications

Physically and mentally fit for the task.
No significant criminal offences or criminal record.
No history of alleged abuse of children, family or partners.
Positive statutory references from police, probation, health and local authorities.
Home meets basic health and safety requirements.
Overall positive personal references.
Stability in personal relationships and circumstances.
No recent significant change in personal circumstances.
No recent significant loss in personal relationships.
Application supported by dependants.
Supportive family, friendship and community network.

Supports and actively promotes the policy on no physical punishment of children and signs the Project's undertaking on child protection.
Undertakes to sign the adopters agreement.

Experience/Knowledge

Hands on experience of looking after children.
Experience of loss or significant changes/upheaval in personal circumstances.
Has a knowledge of standard child development.

Skills / Abilities

Able to form new relationships.
Able to maintain relationships.
Able to command the trust/respect of others.
Demonstrates personal warmth to children and to adults.
Open to new learning.
Values own strengths.
Accepts and builds on feedback.
Can recognise own limitations.
Able to ask for and accept help.
Able to reflect on own experience.
Demonstrates self-discipline.
Is reliable.
Is consistent in approach.
Demonstrates tenacity.
Able to talk about feelings.
Able to talk about difficulties.
Able to listen.
Able to "stand back" from problems.
Able to put a plan into action.
Demonstrates sensitivity to the feelings of others.
Able to see a child's perspective.
Able to discuss issues around sexuality openly.
Able to accept and work with a child's history.

© Barnardo's New Families, Colchester

The participants said their decision to take part in the process centred on the benefits of being with people in the same situation as themselves and the challenge of doing something interesting and different. All but one had taken part before in group programmes through their work situation. Some participants found it more difficult than others to feel part of the group at the beginning. There was consensus that more time should have been spent at the start for participants to get to know each other better in terms of their past histories and reasons for wanting to adopt. The need for more time to help group members relax, make acquaintance and thus participate more in the discussions was found in another study on preparation groups (MacFadyen, 1995).

Visits to the pub to "unwind" after the sessions became the norm, and increasingly participants formed support networks outwith the group, suggesting the need for building in more time for informal contact. After the first few sessions most participants were able to relax and be open with each other, and felt that overall the group was cohesive and worked well together. Among the difficulties reported were members raising issues which were very specific to themselves which took away time from other people, and initial reticence before realising that 'it does not matter if you say something stupid'. One of the single participants felt disadvantaged at not having her sister participate in the group work with her because she saw her sister as closely involved in the adoption plan and as 'the second parent who needed to be educated as well'. Participants thought that the group work should have continued into the matching stage, both to keep the participants informed about each other's progress and to offer support during the difficult stage of waiting for a placement.

There was unanimous agreement that the content of the group work was highly informative and helpful, that participants learned a great deal about child development and were given the opportunity to think seriously and deeply about adoption. There were some criticisms about the over-negative picture presented of adoption and the 'dwelling on problems'. The methods employed such as role play and sculpting were described as enjoyable and good fun. The skills, professionalism and sense of humour of the key workers added to this positive learning experience. The volume of material to read was seen as unrealistic by some, but its usefulness and quality was very much appreciated, and participants thought they would dip into various handouts once they had children placed with them. The break of a month in the middle of the group session and midway meetings with the key worker were perceived by most participants as helpful, particularly in enabling people to reflect as to whether adoption was the right step to take.

This was in fact the point at which one couple decided to withdraw. They felt that without the learning about adoption that happened in the group 'we might not otherwise have pulled out'. They would have found it helpful to have had feedback on the effect on the group of their withdrawal. From the comments of the participants it seems that this did not have too disruptive an effect on the group.

None of the participants had previous experience of writing about themselves in the way required for the Form F. In some this triggered off strong emotions and memories. Responses ranged from it being experienced as therapeutic to having difficulties such as remembering childhood events, not knowing how to deal with 'nasty experiences', having 'not an awful lot to say' and lack of writing experience. Finding time to do the writing was also problematic. Most participants were pleased with their efforts and generally felt they were able to share a great deal of themselves through the Form F, though one couple said they were conscious of what was "politically correct" to include. Comments ranged from 'It's my story and I am proud of it' and 'This is me, you have to be honest with yourself', to 'What you see is what you get'.

The private sessions with the key workers were described as helpful and necessary, giving the opportunity to clarify and elaborate points in the Form F and discuss personal issues. Interestingly, the contribution of the social workers to the Form F was seen as affirming and repeating what the participants had already written about themselves.

The attendance at the adoption panel was described as something of an anti-climax for participants. They had felt anxious at the prospect of coming before the panel and had expected to be in for a "grilling", so were surprised and somewhat disappointed at how short their appearance was. Some thought this was because of 'the experimental nature' of the process. Also, as one participant said, 'it was all there in the writing', leaving little more to be said.

All the participants liked the fact that the process of being approved as adopters was much quicker than in a more conventional assessment. This contrasted with the frustration expressed at the longer time involved for a placement to happen. By the time of the interviews, one couple and one single applicant had been linked with children, but the latter felt this was not right and was subsequently matched with another child. For the rest, waiting for this to happen was difficult to cope with:

We got the impression that there were children in the pipeline.

We expected more offers.

We've done our bit. Where are the children?

Participants were linked to a "waiters' group" for approved adopters waiting for a placement. Some found it helpful 'to meet people in the same boat', but others felt they 'were waiting with nothing to do'. Most of the support was obtained from the participants keeping in touch with each other on an informal basis, and this was expressed as the 'group coming into its own'.

Adoption panel feedback

Interviews were held with three adoption panel members (out of a possible six), who had sat on panels dealing with participants who took part in this new model of assessment. Two of those interviewed were new, both to the self-assessment model and prospective adopters attending adoption panels. The other panel member had some experience of the latter through the membership of another adoption panel in a voluntary adoption agency.

Panel members were very much in favour both of the introduction of self-assessments and of participants presenting the material themselves to the adoption panel. Positives highlighted were the provision of group support and group learning and a shift of responsibility from 'things being done to applicants' to 'taking a strong lead, with social workers in the back seat'. Panel members had no formal training to prepare them for prospective adopters attending the adoption panel. A paper had been written for the panel by the key workers involved with the new model of assessment. After minor adjustments there was agreement to proceed. Panel members were enthusiastic and positive about the experience, stressing the principle of empowerment and the practical benefit of helping panel members to do a more effective job:

It's a fairer process – people taking major decisions should show how they do it.

Adoption should be made an inclusive process as much as possible.

If a worker is raising concerns, we can see applicants addressing it themselves.

While panel members were clear that it was not their job to reassess participants, there was a dilemma as to whether to ask general questions or tackle more sensitive and contentious issues. Overall, the view was that both these areas needed to be addressed – 'You have to keep a balance between not putting people on the spot and not ducking issues.' The experience of taking part in the self-assessment was seen by panel members as helping participants to learn about themselves at the panel. The benefits to panel members of prospective adopters being present were expressed as livelier panels, sharpening practice, being clearer about what they wanted to ask, challenging the panel on what their role was and generally 'helping panels to grow'. Attendance by prospective adopters at adoption panels has now become standard procedure which was very welcomed. At times it was they, rather than panel members, who raised the contentious issues!

One panel member felt that the presence of a prospective adopter at the panel was crucial in moving him away from a negative to a positive view. In this instance, the prospective adopter had written about herself in the third person and used "clichés" which was experienced as distancing. This raised questions in his mind as to 'where this person was emotionally'. In contrast, a strong presentation at the panel positively changed the picture for him. In other cases, panel members were reassured, participants were fleshed out and a three-dimensional picture was obtained.

While some applicants were better than others at writing, panel members said that the quality of the Form F was superior to those written by social workers. It was more interesting and informative, the style and content revealed a lot and there was no jargon – 'it spoke from the heart'. Interestingly though, the adoption panel members still wanted to have the synopsis from the key workers in order to reaffirm what the prospective adopters had written about themselves in the Form F. This may suggest that the strength of the model is in having the key worker assess how prospective adopters assess themselves. On the negative side it could point to anxieties about the redefinition of the professional role to one of a skilled facilitator.

Feedback from the consultant

When the adoption panel originally agreed to the piloting of this model of assessment, they recommended that a consultant be used. Immediately after each group work session the key workers taped a record of what had happened. The transcript was sent to the consultant who then met with the key workers to discuss their observations. Participants knew about the consultant's role and were given feedback on areas of concern and issues that needed further exploration by the key worker.

The consultant observed that the new model helped integrate the theoretical and the personal in a more direct way. This was thought to enable participants to move closer to the reality of older child adoption and focus better on how it would affect them. Another perceived advantage was having two workers throughout, who could lend support to each other and enable them to check out each other's perceptions.

As regards disadvantages of the model, the use of personal experiences in the group work and filling in sections of the Form F might have been too personally and publicly intrusive at an early stage, although participants seemed to cope well with this. The intensity of weekly groups and also having to do formal personal home work between sessions raised the question of whether there was enough time for participants to 'internalise the processes or did it instead take on a task-centred focus which substituted for allowing the internalising work to take place?'. While the consultant was reassured by the key workers that the participants appeared to manage this, she felt that an important task for any workers using this model would be to monitor the process and to slow the pace or make changes if necessary.

Key workers' views

Achieving four to five self-assessments using the new model was more work over a concentrated period of time for the two key workers than undertaking two or three home studies each. No extra resources were made available, there was no reduction in their workload, and it was difficult to get a suitable venue for the group meetings in a central location. As a compensation they were working in a highly motivating and supportive situation, with a co-worker and a consultant. A further advantage was 'not formulating opinions about suitability on their own – it's two views not one view'. The support of the consultant was seen by the key workers as 'luxury' and 'heaven'. It helped to dispel anxieties, to talk and think about the work and to be flexible about changes of direction in the groups. This was found to be a challenging approach in which workers are far more exposed than in the conventional model. The balance of power is not so weighted towards the assessing social worker and efforts are made to demystify the process and explain jargon. Participants put pressure on their key worker to keep to agreed timescales and were annoyed when on two occasions there was a significant delay between submitting the papers to the adoption panel and obtaining a date for hearing the application.

As the process is more speedy in this form of assessment, the waiting for a match between families and children becomes more frustrating. One key worker was surprised at how assertive participants became after their approval as regards matching, as they appeared more able to turn down children for good reasons. While the key workers felt that in some respect they were 'losing power' it is important to remember that real power to recommend participants as adopters was still in their hands and in those of the adoption panel.

Conclusion

We have described an innovative model of self-assessment by adopters combined with group and home work tasks. Participants were enthusiastic about this model. They reported that they had found the experience made a positive contribution to their lives, and boosted their self-confidence and competency in skills such as communication and assertiveness. After approval, strong ties have continued between group members who have supported each other through the matching process and introduced their adopted children to one another. Six children have been placed with the families from the first group – three singleton placements and one sibling group.

We believe this model produces more meaningful assessments which illustrate the qualities of the participants, evidence their understanding of the adoption task and demonstrate their capacity to learn. Self-assessments showed whether applicants could narrate their own history openly, express anger, consistency and coherence. The model of assessment provides demanding but achievable goals which test out their motivation and ability to see tasks through to completion. When participants were approved, it was felt that there was a real measure of the strengths of the resource they were offering.

This model has yet to be tested out in a situation where there is conflict about approval or matching issues between the prospective adopters' self-assessment and the key workers' contribution to the Form F. It is also possible that in this model

prospective adopters could more easily deceive the agency about risk factors in their background, but no model of assessment has guarantees attached to it. It could be argued that the components of this model have additional safeguards: the professional judgment of two workers supported by a consultant, sharing life experiences with other prospective adopters in a group situation, and presenting their self-assessment to the adoption panel.

The model needs further refinement but in essence it represents a significant step forward. It can be used with a wider range of participants than first envisaged, and in a subsequent group there were three childless couples and one couple with a young primary school aged child of their own. Future groups could include second-time around prospective adopters who could make a significant contribution from their experience. As discussed earlier, one single prospective adopter would have preferred to have her closest support person attend the group with her. This also raises issues about how to involve the children of prospective adopters in groups, their contribution to the self-assessment, and attendance at adoption panels.

We would like to continue to develop the practice of self-assessments but consider it vital to do so in close collaboration with the adoption panel, and for panel members to be offered preparation and training for making decisions in relation to this model of assessment.

This article has been reproduced from *Adoption & Fostering*, 22 : 2, 1998.

Assessing Asian Families in Scotland

Satnam Singh

Introduction

A holistic assessment of the needs of children requiring substitute families is paramount not only for a successful placement, by which I mean a placement that does not disrupt, but also for ensuring the psychological well-being of the child.

In Scotland an important aspect of the child's needs has been largely ignored or underplayed by adoption and fostering agencies. I am referring to the identity needs of black children arising from the child's heritage.

As early as 1979, identity formation and identity maintenance were seen as significant tasks for all children in substitute care. In the words of Germaine (1979):

> *The child who must be placed in substitute care at any age, and regardless of the reason, is torn from the biological and symbolic context of his identity. No matter how nurturing the substitute care, the child's ongoing task will always be to reweave the jagged tear in the fabric of his identity, to make himself whole again.*

For black children, however, the denial or whitewash [sic] of the child's heritage has resulted in black children being placed transracially into white substitute families. Consequently, the task of reweaving the fabric of their identity is made all the more difficult.

The "colour-blind" approach to social work which precipitated many of these transracial placements of black children owes much to the prevalent ideology of the late 1970s and early 1980s, when it was believed that black children who identified more closely with white people were actually assimilating successfully and, as such, this was

seen as a sign of psychological well-being. This assimilationist philosophy was derived from a "cultural deficit" model of social work which viewed black people as lacking, abnormal or deviant. In a critique of this view, Rhodes (1992) made explicit the assumptions which were so pervasive throughout the above period:

> *… Black people's life-styles, family patterns and child-rearing practices are deemed inappropriate to life in the modern, advanced Western society … Social workers' role is to preserve the integrity of British cultural values and to facilitate assimilation.*

These melting pot theories also propagated a belief that racism, prejudice and discrimination amounted to a normal and logical reaction to such shortcomings and would necessarily decline once black people fully assimilated into the dominant culture.

Since the 1980s, however, there has been a gradual but significant shift in this thinking due to the influence and struggle of an increasing number of black professionals. This epistemological shift can be traced back to the Association of Black Social Workers and Allied Professionals (ABSWAP), who, in their submission to the House of Commons Select Committee in 1983, wrote that:

> *Bonding without a sense of racial identity is pathological and is against the best interest of the black child.*

Other writers and researchers were also finding evidence to contribute to this emerging ideology. A controversial 1983 study by Gill and Jackson found that transracially placed children only

> *… coped by denying their racial background and had not developed a sense of racial identity – they saw themselves as white in all but skin colour.*

Maximé, writing in the mid-1980s and drawing on her work with black children and adults in care, asserted that black children's misidentification or over-identification with white people was in fact pathological. In a letter to the *Caribbean Times* (18 March 1983), David Divine wrote passionately that this one-way trafficking of black children into white families was the modern-day equivalent of slavery. These children, he stated, are:

> ... *lost to our communities. No community can afford hundreds of such casualties each year, no community can be so profligate with its most precious resources – its children.*

There is – and has been for some time – a clear imperative for action, both from academic sources and from the black communities themselves. This imperative is now further legitimised in Scotland by the requirements of the 1995 Children (Scotland) Act, to take account of a child's racial, cultural, religious and linguistic needs.

The Khandan Initiative

It was in response to these imperatives, coupled with a realisation that in Scotland the needs of black children were remaining unmet, that in 1996 Barnardo's Family Placement Services, an adoption and fostering agency based in Edinburgh, developed the Khandan Initiative. "Khandan" means "family" in Punjabi, Hindi and Urdu, and as such reflects very clearly the nature of the work. Put simply, the Khandan Initiative is trying to attract, recruit and support adoptive and foster carers from the Asian population in the central belt of Scotland.

The primary aim of the Initiative is to ensure that same-race placements are the placements of choice for all children referred to the project for placement in a substitute family. In order for this same-race commitment to become a reality, there are many areas of policy and practice that have changed and continue to change. In the rest of this paper I want to look critically at only one aspect of this process, that of the assessment of Asian families.

Towards an integrated model for the assessment of Asian families

Any discussion about work with black families must give regard to the context in which that work takes place. Dutt (1991) argues that for black people in Britain the context is always of racism.

Racism is such an indelible part of our lives, it permeates everything we do and it affects every interaction and relationship we have.

It was in this context of racism that Nobles (1978) identified that the history of the study of black families is one which has focused primarily on three themes: poverty, pathology and victimisation. Clearly, assessment of black families needs to steer away from these myths which seriously undermine black people and devalue their contribution. Valid assessment of black people needs to move towards a richer understanding of the unique and diverse nature and functioning of black families.

Nobles warned of the danger of "transubstantiation" through a process of "conceptual incarceration" when undertaking assessments of black families. He described transubstantiation as a process 'wherein one defines or interprets the behaviour and/or medium of one culture with the meanings appropriate to another culture'. For example, one aspect of a typical assessment of any family might be to try to establish the quality of the relationships within that family, particularly between the husband and wife. A typical worker might then try to assess this by trying to identify the "behaviours" of the family which relay the "meanings" that the worker is seeking. In a typical white family this might mean such things as holding hands, linking arms, cuddling and spending time in shared leisure activities. It would be fair to say that a typical Asian family would probably not display these behaviours. Being unable to identify the "behaviours" which carry the required "meanings" sought by the worker, the Asian family would then certainly fail the assessment.

Another example of possible misinterpretation could arise from the actual structure and process of the interview itself. In a traditional Asian family the gender roles are very clearly defined. This often results in the wife adopting a much more deferential role in public situations. The interviewer might then find that throughout the interview the wife says very little, perhaps even avoids eye contact, often sitting some distance away from her husband or occasionally with her head slightly down. This behaviour in a traditional interview would probably sit uncomfortably with most social workers. It appears to represent an unequal relationship, where the husband holds and wields the power in the family and where the wife is seen as weak and unassuming. The reality, however, would in most cases be very different with the wife having much more responsibility, autonomy and authority within the context of family, extended family and community. What is being observed is not a negative expression of the quality of the husband's relationship, but rather a manifestation of the values of the family's traditions and culture, in other words, positive attributes.

The process of "conceptual incarceration" is not dissimilar to that of transubstantiation, and is described by Nobles as a process which 'inhibits people from asking the right questions'. Nobles argues that this so-called inhibition occurs as a result of workers having internalised the dominant culture. I would take Nobles' point a stage further and suggest that, even if the right questions are asked, there is a danger of the worker not having the cultural specificity to understand the answers received. For example, most assessment forms ask for information about religion. A recent review of a random selection of assessment forms within our own project showed that the information about religion was either missing, or was so sparse as to be of no value.

Religion may no longer play an important role in the dominant culture, but for many Asian families and communities it is still a significant factor in the ways in which their lives are ordered. A typical social worker may not give this area much significance throughout the assessment process, and thus be culturally inhibited from asking the right questions. Even if questions are asked about the family's religion, what will the social worker do with a response that the family is, for instance, Sikh, Hindu or Muslim? She or he is not likely to have the conceptual framework to interpret the information being received in any meaningful way. As Nobles puts it:

> One's ability to understand black reality is limited if the "interpretive framework" for the analysis of that reality is based on assumptions associated with a non-black reality.

An effective assessment of black families which is both reliable and valid requires a reorientation away from the traditional structures of assessment towards one which seeks to focus on each family's strengths. It is this position, that assessments should focus on a family's strengths, drawn from their social and cultural milieux, which will form the backcloth for the rest of this discussion. (For a useful discussion and checklist of the strengths of black families which provides a reliable tool around which to build an assessment, see Small, 1989.)

Elements of assessment

The traditional assessment focuses on a wide variety of factors, usually including at the very least: childhood, education, health, relationships, work and family. Each of these areas are also of significance in an assessment of Asian families. However, it is my assertion that a valid assessment of Asian families must at the very least take cognisance of four more specific factors:

- the experience of racism;

- marriage as an institution;

- religion and its impact on family functioning; and

- the balance between the family and the self.

The experience of racism

It is important to recognise the impact that the experience of racism has in the way the family functions, about the attitudes and values the family expresses, and the way family life is generally structured on a day-to-day basis. Without a recognition of the centrality of these experiences it is not possible to produce a valid assessment. Without a doubt, the experience of racism will be the single most common feature of every Asian family. This common experience will impinge on every aspect of life, on every member of the family, and on every system and sub-system within that family.

For many individuals the experience of racism will be an inextricable part of their growing up, education, work and leisure throughout their lives in Britain. For others this experience will be amplified by the experiences of loss and change associated with the process of migration. It is important then to ensure that, as these experiences are so central to the existence of Asian people and families, they are not marginalised, side-lined or denied. Instead it is important to recognise the strength, stamina and capacity to flourish and develop in adversity as being positive attributes.

Marriage as an institution

It is probably true to say that the institution of marriage is still of fundamental importance to Asian families and communities, to the extent that its corollary of divorce, separation, adultery and infidelity all exist but are either repressed, denied or not spoken about. Such issues as same-sex relationships are strictly taboo.

The crucial point for an assessment is the recognition that although marriage is "universal", the actual structure, form and meaning vary dramatically across cultures. Most Asian marriages have in the past been arranged, as are many today. These simple words "arranged marriage" carry many racist connotations of young girls being forced against their will to marry older men. The truth of the matter is that "force" and "against their will" are social constructs imposing a reality that does not exist. Marriage within Asian communities, as anywhere else, is a complex social arrangement with subtleties inextricably rooted in culture and history. Marriage is seen not just as a union of two people, but a union of two families. For this union of families to be successful meticulous planning and preparation are required, much of it shrouded in ritual and custom. It is this planning that gives rise to the myth of "arranged".

Marriage is rarely the end product of a long romance, rather the beginning of one. Indeed, romance is rarely seen as a pre-requisite for a successful marriage. In many cases marriages will have taken place abroad, or where one partner is from abroad. Marriages nearly always exist within the context of an extended family and, even where the extended family is fragmented across geographical space, its unity and sanctity remain paramount.

It is clear that in assessments of Asian families, we need to be aware of the many extra dimensions to marriage for it is this richness of marriage as an institution that provides the positive substance and material of assessment.

Religion and its impact on family functioning

Although in the West we live in an increasingly secular society, this contrasts sharply with the role of religion in Asian families for whom it provides many things. Against the backdrop of racism, religion provides a mechanism for affirming and re-affirming identity, not only with other Asians but also with Asian culture and history.

Religion can then be seen as providing meaning, security and continuity in the lives of most Asian families. It also shapes, informs and structures much of their daily lives, by providing rules of conduct, codes of ethics and moral frameworks for interpreting life events. Therefore any proper assessment of Asian families must consider the role of religion in the family's life and how it shapes or influences family functioning. Religion is a central concept to the assessment and should not be confined to a peripheral question to be ticked off on an assessment checklist.

Balance between family and self

The modern world has been described by Lasch (1977) as narcissistic, based as it is on the 'cult of the individual'. He describes the modern personality as shallow, self-centred and lacking emotion. The Asian family, in contrast, does not necessarily place so much importance on the individual. In many cases it is the family or community that is considered to be supreme. It is assumed that either the needs of the individual are one and the same as the needs of the family or group, or that the needs of the individual will be fulfilled when the needs of the family or group are met.

This shift in emphasis in the balance between self and others sits uncomfortably with social work values of promoting independence or empowerment. It is important that assessments take into account that individuals and families do function differently and that at times these may be based on different value systems. Cognisance needs to be given to the way this strong family orientation manifests in the daily functioning of the family and how it is expressed in the family's value system.

Conclusion

It is not possible to be conclusive about what should and should not form part of an assessment. As every worker knows, assessments are as individual as the families being assessed, and we need to be alert to this fact. I have, however, tried to bring together four key elements which must inform any valid assessment of Asian families. Only then can we be sure of identifying the real potential of Asian families in a way that is both relevant to their experiences and that focuses on their particular strengths in a much more meaningful way.

This article has been reproduced from *Adoption & Fostering*, 21 : 3, 1997.

Parents for Children

Karen Irving
Parents for Children

Twenty two years ago, Parents for Children was launched as a pioneering specialist agency to test out whether older and severely disabled children could be placed with permanent alternative families.

It started with a small team of people and although it is three times the size it was, it remains small. It stays small because in our view a small, highly trained, focussed and well supported team is what it takes to place children of exceptional need in a new family and to ensure that the child remains with the new family. We rarely work with more than 20 children at a time. The children referred to us have often had many failed family placements. Some years we place twenty or more children, some years as few as six. It is this focus which has enabled us to establish what works for us in finding families for the most challenging children.

When we do make a new family, it usually works for life. We have a breakdown or disruption rate of below five per cent.

Our model of adoption is simple. Each child is a unique "project" and from the moment we begin our work we tailor-make a programme designed to find the family for that child. We do not have a "pool of waiting adopters". In our view you cannot prepare a family for a notional child. It is too abstract. We wait for a family to "choose" their child from publicity we generate or the photo-sheets we send them and if the Brown family choose Peter, this will include his likes and dislikes (we have yet to come across a child who chooses liver or mushrooms as a favourite food!), his hobbies, and all the good news about Peter's potential. And yes, all the bad news about Peter's

history and what he does when he is under stress, urinating on the bedroom carpet or when he is angry, smearing his faeces. His lying, stealing and sexually provocative behaviour. The Brown family hear about all of this. If they remain committed to Peter, we will be committed to them and put in the supports that help make placements stick.

Each child is unique, yes, but after 22 plus years we have learned a great deal about what helps families and children keep going through the rough and smooth of becoming a new family.

We know that the key component in our work is the trust the families have in us. We are there to assist, not to intrude, not to blame, not to patronise. Because we are small, families know who we are and they know we are there for them. It used to be a house rule that each letter we received, each telephone message was responded to the very same day it was received. We cannot always keep that promise today (we have placed hundreds of children with hundreds of families) but we are still speedy at responding to a request.

We use a paging system to provide out of hours support. Families feel able to use it. It works well.

The placement of Peter in his new family is just the tip of the iceberg: 40 per cent of the work happens before the child is placed, 60 per cent happens afterwards. It is the post-placement and post-adoption work which is in many ways the key to success.

Our families so often tell us, 'You told us what it would be like but we didn't really understand until we lived with Peter's feelings'.

Describing the reality of living with a child who has been neglected, abused physically and sexually, and subjected to the vicissitudes of the care system is an impossible task. 'Like trying to pin an amoeba to a wall,' said a colleague. What we do know of such a child is that his world is perceived as miserable, untrustworthy, painful, yes, evil. That is the world he tries to recreate in his new family. We know that his new mother (it is usually the mother) will be made to feel worthless, ruthless and persecuting. Her partner (if this is a two parent family) will be tempted to disbelieve the descriptions of the child's vile behaviour for when he returns home he sees a sweet, smiling well behaved sorrowful little mite. Not the monstrous creature who emerges when he is away from the home.

It is perfectly possible for a sweet faced six-year old-girl to wreak havoc in her new family. We have seen it happen again and again. But we have also built up a repertoire of manoeuvres, practical and theoretical, that help the family to tame, little by little, the most persistent demons which torment a child.

What we do is "hold" the family through that process. We listen, we advise, we support practically with a rapidly developing respite service. We teach our families new ways of coping or we find experts who can. We observe and often remind our families of the progress apparent to us but not so readily observable to them.

Today we face a new and even more complex challenge. Today's hard to place children come to us with a long, tortuous and seemingly unremitting history of abuse, dislocation and trauma. And increasingly, drug abuse. And, inevitably, of failure.

Alongside our model of family placement, we also have a broad strategy which involves a whole programme of care, befriending and support for the child and the family, respite care, counselling, therapeutic provision and a network of peer support.

While obviously building a team of highly experienced social workers is important, we also include in the team people from other disciplines such as occupational therapy, nursing or clinical psychology. We are able to call upon our consultants, a child psychiatrist, an educational psychologist, an analytical psychologist and therapist. These people work with the families and the children as well as advising us.

Family placement for older, disturbed children is highly skilled work requiring enormous attention to detail. Families adopting such children need a service which supports them and their children for many years. But family placement, if it works, and our low disruption rate shows it can work, is a far cheaper option for society in the longer term. The children who are failed by the care system are the young people sleeping rough in our major cities and the drug and alcohol addicted and mentally ill of tomorrow's world. Such desolate people have been deprived of an opportunity to become part of humankind – their distress is visible to us all. If we are to tackle this problem we need to be able to argue for the resources it needs and lobby for recognition of the demands of the task.

Positive Parenting Skills in Post Adoption Work

Maria Shortis and Jadwiga Ball

Aims and Objectives

The Catholic Children's Society in Bristol has over the past year offered workshops to adoptive parents in parenting skills as a means of post adoption support for families.

The overall aim of the parenting course is to help parents identify and use the parenting skills that work for them in their role as adoptive parents, and to provide an opportunity for peer support in a safe and confidential environment. Our objective is to enable parents to gain self-confidence, to value themselves as "good enough" and to develop their own style of parenting, and self- confidence.

Criteria

None of the social workers involved in the placements of children take part in the parenting skills courses. This gives parents opportunity for mutual support and avoids the pitfall of anyone being seen as having the "expert" role. All families continue to have social work support as individually agreed.

The group was open to all adoptive parents who had children placed in the previous 12 months. The age range of the children was 3 years to 11 years, including sibling groups.

A qualified trainer in adult education, with specific experience in parenting and communication skills, facilitates the group. It is co-led by an adoptive parent who has had considerable experience in facilitating parenting programmes for the past four years in her own community.

Structure

Due to the geographical area covered by the Adoption Society, it was decided to hold workshop days for parents on a monthly basis.

The day followed a structured programme and ran from 10 am – 4 pm. It was divided into two sessions, morning and afternoon.

The morning session provided a safe environment for parents to download about their own personal journey through the adoption process and to exchange views with other parents.

The afternoon session focussed on the use of practical parenting skills and ideas to support both parents and child/children.

The adoptive parent facilitator led the afternoon session with the trainer as co-leader.

In between the two sessions the group broke for lunch and continued to interact. During the subsequent months the lunch became an important focus of sharing and nurturing and it continues to play a significant part in the workshop.

Course materials

The course materials we are using in these workshops come from the Family Caring Trust. They cover a range of parenting programmes such as the Five to Fifteen's Basic Parenting Programme, Parenting Assertiveness, Parenting Teenagers and Parenting and Sex. The materials have been used by more than 100,000 parents during the past three years throughout the United Kingdom.

We have been using these course materials since 1990 within the local community, in schools, homes, and health centres, and have seen the development and growth and introduction of new courses such as the Pram to Primary Course.

The Pram to Primary Course is aimed at children from 0–6 years of age. We are using it because we recognise that, for parents whose children have been placed during the past 12 months, relationships and parenting skills are still being established.

One of the main reasons for using these materials is that they challenge parents to look at their own experience of being parented. They allow parents to take a step back and begin to change learned patterns of behaviour so that their children will receive parenting which is informed, aware, and thoughtful.

Again, the course materials do not seek to provide instant solutions. They aim to make parents think through the challenges of parenting with greater emphasis on how to avoid taking the emotional bait. It is a bit like going to a gym to lose weight. As most people are aware there is no benefit from crash dieting, but there is great benefit from regular working out.

So this is real parenting training and there are pitfalls and there are failures and there are challenges, but the perspective is on practising the skills and learning to change inflexible, ingrained patterns of behaviour that are of no benefit to the children we care for. It encourages parents to recognise just how many skills they do have and to be confident in using the strategies that work for them.

The focus is also on enabling children to experience respect and to learn how to show respect in their families. Challenging behaviour is covered with emphasis on giving positive attention when it is least expected and ignoring as much misbehaviour as is safe to do. The reasoning for this is to avoid creating a pathology or labelling a child, which invariably results in a continuing cycle of destructive and discouraging behaviour.

Finally, the course teaches us much about dealing with and safely expressing feelings. Frustration and anger are almost always about the child's own view of him/herself and mask the pain and hurt underlying the feelings.

By learning to get underneath the expressed behaviour through active listening (and how many of us actually do it?) we can give a child a unique experience of being understood, which is therapeutic and healing.

Having worked with these programmes in the local community for over eight years, and using

them in groups with parents whose children have particular challenging behaviour, we have seen tremendous benefit for both children and parents.

Parenting Skills courses are not viewed by the Society as a one-off event, or a panacea for all ills. They are seen as a rolling programme and an intrinsic part of post adoption support for parents from the time their children are placed through to the teen years and beyond.

Feedback

By listening to the parents who have attended the workshops, we have made some changes by request. We have had to shorten the day by two hours so that parents can get back in time to pick up their children from school. This means the workshop now runs from 10 am – 2 pm. Lunch is seen as an important part of the workshop. The rest of the time is now more concentrated, but not rushed. The group is cohesive but pleased to welcome new parents as placements are made. It is clear from feedback we receive that parents value this group.

One of the most frequent comments has been that the group provides 'an opportunity to talk freely with other parents who understand'.

Other comments include:

It is wonderful to share and hear similar experiences and no longer feel so isolated.

The video is thought provoking.

The course handbook gives you a feeling of safety as it is yours to keep.

I know I am a better person for coming to this group.

When I think about the choices the parenting course offers me I can stand back and give my daughter a choice rather than rushing into a power struggle with her.

It has made me a more confident parent and has made me think about how I was parented

and that I can break the unhelpful patterns by
working on the skills.

Summary

The group will continue to meet monthly and the workshops will run on a rolling programme so that parents feel enabled to join at any point, and are not put under unnecessary pressure if they miss a session.

A course also runs for parents of adopted teenagers and is facilitated in the same manner as above, but takes place in the evenings.

Appendix IV

BAAF and other useful organisations

BAAF and BAAF services

British Agencies for Adoption and Fostering (BAAF)

BAAF is a registered charity and professional association for all those working in the child care field. BAAF's work includes giving advice and information to members of the public on aspects of adoption, fostering and child care issues; publishing a wide range of books, training packs and leaflets as well as a quarterly journal on adoption, fostering and child care issues; providing training and consultancy services to social workers and other professionals to help them improve the quality of medical, legal and social work services to children and families; giving evidence to government committees on subjects concerning children and families; responding to consultative documents on changes in legislation and regulations affecting children in or at risk of coming into care; and helping to find new families for children through BAAF*Link* and *Be My Parent*.

Be My Parent

Every two months, about 300 children waiting for new permanent families are featured in *Be My Parent*, the national family-finding newspaper published by BAAF. Subscribers to *Be My Parent* include already approved adopters, those waiting to be approved, and those who have only just begun to think about adopting or permanently fostering. Children of all ages and with a wide range of needs from all over the country are featured, and therefore *Be My Parent* seeks as wide a readership as possible.

Many hundreds of families (married couples and single people) adopted after first having seen their child's photograph and read their profile in *Be My Parent*. It is easy to subscribe and have the

newspaper sent directly to you – just telephone the number below. If you see children in *Be My Parent* who you would like to become part of your family, one telephone call to our staff will begin the process that could lead to you becoming approved to adopt that child.

For people already approved to adopt or permanently foster children of five and under, BAAF also publishes *Focus on Fives*. This newsletter, circulated to subscribers fortnightly, is available in the same way.

Be My Parent is at
BAAF
Skyline House
200 Union Street
London SE1 OLX
Tel: 0171 593 2060/1/2
FAXl: 0171 593 2001

BAAF*Link*

BAAF*Link* is a national database of children and families referred by local authorities and voluntary adoption agencies throughout Britain. Details of children needing permanent new families and of families approved by agencies are stored and links are made between the two.

BAAF*Link* seeks a variety of approved families for children needing permanent placements – couples and single people, older people and those with or without children who can reflect the cultural and religious needs of children of all ages. We particularly need black families, especially those of African-Caribbean and Asian descent, and couples in which one partner is white and one African-Caribbean. Any family referred to BAAF*Link* must be approved to adopt or permanently foster.

BAAF*Link* is at:
MEA House
Ellison Place
Newcastle-upon-Tyne NE1 8XS
Tel: 0191 232 3200
Fax: 0191 232 2063

Scottish Resource Network

The Scottish Resource Network is a child placement service run by BAAF in Scotland. The West of Scotland Consortium facilitates the placement of children across local authority boundaries in Scotland. Information about the Scottish Resource Network and West of Scotland Consortium can be obtained from the Scottish Centre (see below).

BAAF Offices

More information about BAAF can be obtained from:

HEAD OFFICE
Skyline House
200 Union Street
London SE1 OLX
Tel: 0171 593 2000
Fax: 0171 593 2001

SCOTTISH CENTRE
40 Shandwick Place
Edinburgh EH2 4RT
Tel: 0131 225 9285
Fax: 0131 226 3778

WELSH CENTRE
7 Cleeve House
Lambourne Crescent
Cardiff CF4 5GJ
Tel: 01222 761155
Fax: 01222 747934

ENGLAND
Southern Region
Skyline House
200 Union Street
London SE1 OLX
Tel: 0171 593 2041/2
Fax: 0171 593 2001 (Head Office fax)

Central and Northern Region
St George's House
Coventry Road
Coleshill
Birmingham B46 3EA
Tel: 01675 463 998
Fax: 01675 465 620

and at

Grove Villa
82 Cardigan Road
Headingley
Leeds LS6 3BJ
Tel: 0113 274 4797
Fax: 0113 278 0492

and at

MEA House
Ellison Place
Newcastle-upon-Tyne NE1 8XS
Tel: 0191 261 6600
Fax: 0191 232 2063
.

Organisations for parents

AFAA
(The Association for Families who have Adopted Abroad)

AFAA
89 Upper Fant Road
Maidstone
Kent ME16 8BT

Contact a Family

Contact a Family is a national charity for any parent or professional involved with or caring for a child with disabilities. Through a network of mutual support and self-help groups, Contact a Family brings together families whose children have disabilities, and offers advice and information to parents who wish to start a support group.

Contact a Family
170 Tottenham Court Road
London W1P 0HA
Tel: 0171 383 3555
Fax: 0171 383 0259

Exploring Parenthood

Exploring Parenthood is an organisation which offers help and advice to parents and runs an advice line during office hours.

Exploring Parenthood
4 Ivory Place
20a Treadgold Street
London W11 4BP
Tel: 0171 221 6681
Fax: 0171 221 5501

Parent Network

Parent Network is a national charity that offers a range of courses to parents and professionals supporting families. Courses aim to enhance skills and relationships within the family, using positive, but non-violent approaches to discipline.

Parent Network
Winchester House
11 Cranmer Road
London SW9 6EJ
Tel: 0171 735 1214
Fax: 0171 735 4692

Parent to Parent Information on Adoption Services (PPIAS)

now called *Adoption UK* is a self-help support and information service for adoptive families and prospective adopters with local support groups and contacts all over the UK. A quarterly journal, *Adoption Today* (formerly *Adoption UK*), information leaflets and resource packs are available to all members.

Membership £15 per annum

Lower Boddington
Daventry
Northants NN11 6YB
Tel: 01327 260295

Post and after adoption centres

There are many well established after adoption services now that provide a service for adoptive families, adopted people and birth parents whose children were adopted. Many of them offer advice and counselling, preferably in person, but also on the telephone or by correspondence, for individuals and families. Some also organise events which focus on matters related to adoption, and provide the opportunity for people to meet in common interest groups.

Post-Adoption Centre
Torriano Mews
Torriano Ave
London NW5 2RZ
Tel:0171 284 0555

After Adoption Wales
Unit 1 Cowbridge Court
58-62 Cowbridge Road
West Cardiff CF5 5BS
Tel: 01222 565 318

Merseyside Adoption Centre
316-317 Coopers Building
Church Street
Liverpool L1 3AA
Tel: 0151 709 9122

After Adoption
12-14 Chapel Street
Salford
Manchester M3 7NN
Tel: 0161 839 4930

West Midlands Post Adoption Service (WMPAS)
92 Newcombe Road
Handsworth
Birmingham B21 8DD
Tel: 0121 523 3345

Family Care
21 Castle Street
Edinburgh
EH2 3DN Tel: 0131 225 6441

After Adoption Yorkshire
82 Cardigan Road
Leeds LS6 3B5
Tel: 0113 230 2100

Barnardo's Scottish Adoption Advice Service
16 Sandyford Place
Glasgow G3 7NB
Tel: 0141 339 1772

Local authorities may also provide help and support. In Scotland, they have a duty to help adoptive families, adopted children and birth families. They sometimes use the help of voluntary agencies for this.

Fostering

National Foster Care Association (NFCA)
87 Blackfriars Road
London SE1 8HA
Tel: 0171 620 6400

NFCA Scotland
1 Melrose Street
Queens Crescent
Glasgow G4 9BJ
Tel: 0141 204 1400

Other Organisations

ISSUE

ISSUE is the national self-help organisation which provides information, support and representation to people with fertility difficulties and those who work with them.

Membership £30 for first year
Then £20 per annum,
£7.50 low income

ISSUE
114 Litchfield Street
Walsall WS1 1SZ
Tel: 01922 722 888

The National Organisation for Counselling Adoptees and their Parents (NORCAP)

NORCAP is a self-help support group for all parties to adoption. It helps adult adopted people to get in touch with their birth parents, as well as offering help and support to birth parents, adoptive parents, and siblings of adopted people. NORCAP maintains a successful Contact Register and publishes a regular newsletter three times a year.

Annual subscription £25.00 including registration (first year); registration £5.00, membership renewal £15.00

Members receive a newsletter three times per year and can buy other publications.

NORCAP
Church Road
Wheatley
Oxon OX33 1LU
Tel: 01865 875000

Overseas Adoption Helpline

The Overseas Adoption Helpline offers advice and information about current policy and practice in relation to overseas adoption and the legal requirements of the UK and sending countries.

Overseas Adoption Helpline
PO Box 13899
London N6 4WB
Tel: 0990 168742

Family Caring Trust

Family Caring Trust
44 Rathfriland Road
Newry, Co Down BT34 1LD
Tel: 01693 64174

For information about Parenting Courses/Community Programmes on Support for Parenting.

Joseph Rowntree Foundation
The Homestead
40 Water End
York YO30 6WP
Tel: 01904 629241

For information about Findings series.

Videos

Some agencies have already made videos of individual children awaiting placement, others have brought together groups like older adoptees or experienced families to make their own videos. While they may not attain the quality or professionally produced videos, social workers should consider creative use of technology to widen their resources.

Addresses for videos –
BBC Videos for Education & Training
Room A2025, Woodlands
80 Wood Lane
London W12 0TT
Tel: 0181 576 2541

Concorde Video & Film Council
201 Felixstowe Road
Ipswich IP3 9BJ

REFERENCES

ABSWAP (1983) *Black children in care*, Evidence to the House of Commons Social Services Committee.

Ahmed, S. (1981) 'Children in care: the racial dimension in social work assessment', in Cheetham, J., Loney, M., Mayor, B. and Prescott, W. (eds) *Social and Community Work in a Multi-racial Society*, London: Harper & Row.

Archer, C. (1999) *Parenting the child who hurts: the first steps*, London: Jessica Kingsley.

Archer, C. (1999) *Parenting the hurt child : the next steps*, London: Jessica Kingsley.

Argent, H. (1998) *Whatever Happened to Adam?*, London: BAAF.

Argent, H. (ed) (1995) *See You Soon: Contact with looked after children*, London: BAAF.

Axline, V. (1964) *Dibs in Search of Self*, London: Penguin.

BAAF (1999) *Contact in Permanent Placement*, Good Practice Guide, London: BAAF.

Baffour, S. (1999) 'A black adoptive carer's perspective', in Barn, R., *Working with Black Children and Adolescents in Need*, London: BAAF.

Barn, R. (1999) 'Racial and ethnic identity', in Barn, R., *Working with Black Children and Adolescents in Need*, London: BAAF.

Barnardo's, *Networks*, Video

Barrett, J. H. W. (1998) 'New knowledge and research in child development – research reviews', in *Child and Family Social Work*, 3 : 4, pp 267-276.

Bayard, R. T. and Bayard, J. (1990) *'Help – I've got a teenager: A survival guide for desperate parents'*, Exley Publications.

BBC, *Bringing up Baby*, Video

BBC, *Challenging Behaviour*, Video.

Bearman, F. (1993) *Surviving Five*, Barnardo's, Scotland.

* Berridge, D. and Cleaver, H. (1987) *Foster Home Breakdown*, Oxford: Blackwell.

Bingley-Miller, L. and McNeish, D. (1993) 'Paramountcy or partnership? Applicants attending adoption panel', in *Adoption & Fostering*, 17 : 4, pp 15-22.

Bolam, L. (May 1995) 'The adopted child at school', in *Adoption UK*, No. 73.

Bowlby, J. (1988) *A Secure Base: Clinical application of attachment theory*, London: Tavistock/Routlege.

* Bretherton, E. and Waters, E. (eds) (1985) *Growing Points of Attachment Theory and Research*, Monograph of the Society for Research in Child Development, Vol 50, Nos 1-2, Chicago: University of Chicago Press, USA.

Briere, J. (1992) *Child Abuse Trauma: Theory and Treatment of the Lasting Effects*, Sage.

Brodzinsky, D. and Schechter, M. (1990) *The Psychology of Adoption*, Oxford: Oxford University Press.

Bullock, R., Little, M. and Millham, S. (1993) *Going Home: The return of children separated from their families*, Dartmouth Publishing Co.

Burnell, A. 'His, Hers and Theirs – A Post Adoption Perspective on Gender Issues', Post Adoption Centre.

Burnell, A. (1990) 'Explaining Adoption to children who have been adopted – how do we find the right words?', Discussion paper, London: Post Adoption Centre

Burnell, A., Dagoo, R., Sitsel, A. and Reich, D. (1993) *Thoughts on Adoption: By black adults adopted by white parents*, London: Post Adoption Centre.

Burnell, A., Reich, D. and Sawbridge, P. (eds) (1992) *Infertility and Adoption*, Discussion papers, London: Post Adoption Centre.

Burnham, J. (1986) *Family Therapy – First Steps Towards a Systemic Approach*, London: Tavistock.

Campbell, J. (November 1994) 'The impact of the past', in *Adoption UK*, No. 71.

Channel 4, *Baby It's You*, Video.

Cheetham, J. (1982) 'Problems of adoption for black children', in Cheetham, J. (ed) *Social Work and Ethnicity,* London: National Institute of Social Work.

Chennells, P. and Morrison, M. (1998) *Talking About Adoption,* London: BAAF.

* Child Welfare Institute (1992) *Group Preparation and Selection,* USA.

Clark, I., McWilliam, E. and Phillips, R. (1998) 'Empowering Prospective Adopters' in *Adoption & Fostering*, 22 : 2.

Clulow, C. (ed) (1996) *Partners Becoming Parents,* London: Sheldon Press.

Concorde Videos, *A Class Divided*.

Concorde Videos, *Being White*.

Cudmore, L. 'The Impact of Infertility on the Couple Relationship', Post Adoption Centre.

Dickson, V. (1995) 'A care leaver's perspective of care and contact', in Argent, H. (ed) *See You Soon: Contact with looked after children*, London: BAAF.

Divine, D. (1983) 'Time for decision', in *The Caribbean Times,* 18 March.

Douglas, C. (1996) 'A model assessment and matching' in Phillips, R. & McWilliam, E. (eds) *After Adoption: Working with adoptive families,* London: BAAF.

Dubois, D. (1987) 'Preparing applicants in Wandsworth', in *Adoption & Fostering*, 11 : 2, pp 35-37.

Dutt, R. (1991) 'Open adoption – a black perspective', in *Adoption & Fostering,* 15 : 4, p111.

Erikson, E. H. (1963) *Childhood and Society,* London: Penguin.

Fahlberg, V. (1994) *A Child's Journey through Placement,* London: BAAF.

Farnfield, S. (1998) 'Attachment and the care of looked after children in their middle years', in *Exchanging Visions*, London: BAAF.

Fitzgerald, J. (Revised 1990) *Understanding Disruption,* London: BAAF.

Fratter, J. (1996) *Adoption with Contact – Implications for Policy and Practice,* London: BAAF.

Gaber, I. and Aldridge, J. (eds) (1994) *In the Best Interests of the Child: Culture, identity and transracial adoption,* London: Free Association Books.

Germaine, C. B. (1979) 'Social work practice: people and environment', in Maluccio, A., Fein, E. and Olmstead, K. (1986) *Permanency Planning for Children: Concepts and methods,* London: Tavistock.

Gill, O. and Jackson, B. (1983) *Adoption and Race: Black, Asian and mixed race children in white families,* London: Batsford/BAAF.

Gilligan, R. (1997) 'Beyond Permanence? The importance of resilience in child placement practice and planning', in *Adoption & Fostering* 21 : 1.

Gottman, J. M. (1997) *Why Marriages Succeed or Fail,* London: Bloomsbury.

Gutridge, P. (May 1995) 'Fatherhood, fathering and adoption', in *Adoption UK*, No. 73.

Harrison, M. (November 1996) 'Dilemma', a poem, *Adoption UK,* No. 79.

Hender, P. (1994) 'Applicants attending local authority adoption panels', in *Adoption & Fostering,* 18 : 1, pp 45-48.

Hess, P. M. and Proch, K. O. (1993) *Contact: Managing visits to children,* London: BAAF.

Hicks, M. and McDermott, J. (1999) *Lesbian and Gay Fostering and Adoption,* London: Jessica Kingsley.

HMSO (1991) *Family Placement – Guidance and Regulations,* Vol 3, London: HMSO.

HMSO (1995) *The Children (Scotland) Act,* London: HMSO.

HMSO (1998) *Achieving the Right Balance,* London: HMSO.

Hoffman, L. (1991) 'A reflective stance for family therapy', in *Journal of Strategic and Systemic Therapies,* 10 : 4-17.

Horne, J. & Haunton, A. (1994) *Applicants at Panel,* Barnardo's.

Horne, J. (1981) 'Group work with adopters', in *Adoption & Fostering,* 106 : 4, pp 21-25.

Howe, D. (1995) 'Adoption and attachment', in *Adoption & Fostering,* 19 : 4.

Howe, D. (1995) *Attachment Theory for Social Work Practice,* London: Macmillan.

Howe, D. (1996) *Adopters on Adoption: Reflections on parenthood and children,* London: BAAF.

Howe, D. (1997) *Patterns of Adoption*, Blackwell Science.

Jewett, C. (1994) *Helping Children Cope with Separation and Loss,* London: Batsford/BAAF.

Joseph Rowntree Trust (1998) *Children's Perspectives on Families, Research findings,* London: Joseph Rowntree Trust.

Kaniuk, J. (1996) 'Mental health issues for children and families: the perspectives from a placing agency', in *BAAF AGM Seminar Papers*, London: BAAF.

Katz, I., Spoone-More, N. and Robinson, C. (1994) *Concurrent Planning: From permanency planning to permanency action,* Washington: Lutheran Social Services of Washington and Idaho, USA.

Klaus, M. H. and Kennell, J. H. (1976) *Maternal-Infant Bonding*, C V Mosby Company, USA.

* Laing (1995) [on page 25, App III 4]

Lasch, C. (1977) *Haven in a Heartless World: The family besieged,* New York: Basic Books, USA.

Laycock, F., Thorley, J. Schatzberger, R. (1987) 'A team approach to foster parent assessment', in *Adoption and Fostering,* 7 : 4.

Leach, P. (1997) *Getting Positive about Discipline: A guide for today's parents,* London: Barnardo's and The National Early Years Network.

Lord, J., Barker, S. and Cullen, D. (1997) *Effective Panels,* London: BAAF.

MacFayden, S. (1995) 'Preparing or deterring? Consumer feedback on preparation groups for prospective adoptive parents in Barnardo's Family Placement Project, Edinburgh', in Fuller, R. and Petch, A. *Practitioner Research – The reflexive social worker,* Buckingham: Open University Press.

Macliver, C. and Thom, M. (1990) *Family Talk,* London: BAAF.

Main, M. 'Cross-cultural studies of attachment organisation: recent studies, changing methodologies and the concept of conditional strategies', in *Human Development,* 33 pp 48-61.

Main, M. and Goldwyn, R. (1984) 'Predicting rejection of her infant from mother's representation of her own experience: implications for the abused-abusing inter-generational cycle.' in *Child Abuse and Neglect,* Vol 8 pp203-17.

Maluccio, A., Fein, E. and Olmstead, K. (1986) *Permanency Planning for Children: Concepts and methods,* London: Tavistock.

Masson, H. C. (1984) *Applying Family Therapy: A practical guide for social workers,* London: Pergamon Press.

Maximé, J. (1991) 'Some psychological models of black self-concept' in Ahmed, S., Cheetham, J. and Small, J. (eds), *Social Work with Black Children and their Families,* London: Batsford/BAAF.

McKenna, M. (1989) *What makes a good adoptive parent?,* MSc dissertation, University of Stirling.

McKenzie-Mavinga, I. and Perkins, T. (1991) *In Search of Mr McKenzie: Two sisters' quest for an unknown father,* London: The Women's Press.

McLoughlin, C. (February 1995) 'Denying contact is wrong', in *Adoption UK,* No. 72.

McNamara, J., Bullock, A. and Grimes, E. (1995) *Bruised before Birth,* London: BAAF.

Monroe, C. (1993) *The Child Within,* London: The Children's Society.

Munnoch, S. (November 1995) 'When parents cannot bond', in *Adoption UK,* No. 75.

NFCA, *Caring for the sexually abused child*, Video.

NFCA (1994) *Safe Caring*, NFCA.

Nobles, W. (1978) 'Toward an empirical and theoretical framework for defining black families', in *Journal of Marriage and the Family*, 70, pp 679-88.

Overett, J. (1998, unpublished) *Substitute Families – Assessing the risk of child sexual abuse*, Barnardo's.

Owen, M. (1999) *Novices, Old Hands and Professionals: Adoption by single people*, London: BAAF.

Part, D. (1993) 'Fostering as seen by carers of children', in *Adoption & Fostering*, 17 : 20.

Perry, B. (1993) 'Neurodevelopment and the neurophysiology of trauma', in *The APSAC Advisor*, vol 6 1 & 2.

Phillips, R. & McWilliam, E. (eds) (1996) *After Adoption: Working with adoptive families*, London: BAAF.

Prevatt Goldstein, B. 'Direct work with black children with one white parent', in Barn, R. (1999).

Pugh G, (1996) 'Seen but not heard? Addressing the needs of children who foster', in *Adoption & Fostering*, 20 : 1.

Quinton, D. *et al* (1997) 'Contact between children placed away from home and their birth parents; research issues and evidence', in *Child Psychology and Psychiatry*, 2 : 3.

Randolph, E. (1997) *Children Who Shock and Surprise*, RFR Publications, USA.

Raphael-Leff, J. 'Transition to Parenthood – Infertility', Post Adoption Centre.

Rashid, S. (1996) 'Attachment reviewed through a cultural lens', in Howe, D. (ed) *Attachment and Loss in Child and Family Social Work*, Aldershot: Avebury.

Reich, D. 'Family creation: The continuing impact of infertility', in *Infertility and Adoption, Discussion papers*, London: Post Adoption Centre.

Reimers, S. and Treacher, A. (1995) *Introducing User-Friendly Family Therapy*, London: Routledge.

Research Review (1997) 'Forming Fresh Attachments in Childhood: A research update', in *Child and Family Social Work*, 2, pp121-127.

Rhodes, P. (1992) *Racial Matching in Fostering*, Aldershot: Avebury.

Rosenberg, E. B. (1992) *The Adoption Life Cycle*, The Free Press.

Ryan, T. and Walker, R. (1999) *Life Story Work*, 2nd edition, London: BAAF .

Ryburn, M. (1991) 'The myth of assessment', in *Adoption & Fostering*, 15 : 1, pp 21-27.

Ryburn, M. (1995) 'Adopted children's identity and information needs', in *Children and Society*, 9 : 3, pp 41-64.

Sellick, C. & Thoburn, J. (1996) *What Works in Family Placement?*, Essex: Barnardo's.

Selwyn, J. (1991) 'Applying to adopt: the experience of rejection?', in *Adoption & Fostering*, 15 : 3, pp 227-29.

Selwyn, J. (1994) 'Spies, informers and double agents – adoption assessments and role ambiguity', in *Adoption & Fostering*, 18 : 4, pp 43-7.

Singh, S. (1997) 'Assessing Asian families in Scotland – a discussion', in *Adoption & Fostering*, 21 : 3, pp 35-9. Also reproduced in Appendices.

Sjögren, J. S. (1996) 'A ghost in my country', in *Adoption & Fostering*, 20 : 2.

Sjögren, J. S. (1997) 'Dreams end', in *Adoption & Fostering*, 21 : 2.

Small, J. (1989) 'Transracial placements: conflicts and contradictions', in Morgan, S. and Righton, P. (eds) *Child Care: Concerns and conflicts*, London: Hodder & Stoughton.

Small, J. (1991) 'Ethnic and racial adoption within the United Kingdom', in *Adoption & Fostering*, 15 : 4, pp 61-9.

Smith, C. (1984) *Adoption and Fostering: Why and how,* London: Macmillan.

Smith, G. (1995) 'Do children have the right to leave their past behind them' in Argent, H. (ed) *See You Soon: Contact with looked after children,* London: BAAF.

Smith, G. (1995) *The Protector's Handbook,* London: The Women's Press.

Smith, S. (1994) *Learning from Disruption: Making better placements,* London: BAAF.

Social Services Inspectorate (1995) *Moving Goal Posts: A study of post adoption contact in the north of England*, Department of Health.

Social Services Inspectorate (1996) *For Children's Sake*, Department of Health.

Sparks, K. (1995) *Why Adoption?: Experiences to share for teenagers and their adoptive parents,* London: BAAF.

Steele, M., Kaniuk, J., Hodges, J., Haworth, C. and Huss, S. (1999) 'The use of the adult attachment interview: implications for assessment in adoption and foster care' in *Assessment: Preparation and Support*, London: BAAF.

Steele, M., Hodges, J., Kaniuk, J., Henderson, K., Hillman, S. and Bennett, P. (1999) 'The use of story stem narratives in assessing the inner world of the child: implications for adoptive placements' in *Assessment: Preparation and Support*, London: BAAF.

Stevenson, P. (1991) 'A model of self-assessment for prospective adopters', in *Adoption & Fostering,* 15 : 3, pp 30-4.

Stratton, P., Preston-Shoot, M., Hanks, H. (1990) *Family Therapy: Training and practice,* Venture Press.

* Thoburn, J. (1994) *Child Placement: Principles and practice*, Ashgate.

Trent, J. (1990) *Applicants at Panel,* Barnardo's.

Triseliotis, J., Shineman, J. and Hundleby, M. (1997) *Adoption: Theory, policy and practice*, Cassell.

Triseliotis, J. (1988) 'Introduction to the preparation and selection of adoptive and foster parents', in Triseliotis, J. (ed) *Group Work in Adoption and Foster Care,* London: Batsford.

Triseliotis, J. Sellick, C. and Short, R. (1995) *Foster Care: Theory and practice,* London: Batsford.

Van Gulden, H. and Bartels-Rabb, L. (1995) *Real Parents, Real Children,* New York: The Crossroads Publishing Company, USA.

Verity, P. (1995) 'Foster carers and contact', in Argent, H. (ed) *See You Soon: Contact with looked after children,* London: BAAF.

Verrier, N. (1993) *The Primal Wound,* Baltimore: Gateway Press, USA.

Walrond-Skinner, S., Watson, D. (eds) (1987) *Ethical Issues in Family Therapy,* London: Routledge Kegan Paul.

Wells, S. (1994) 'One Family's Experience of Contact', in *Adoption UK*, No. 68.

Westacott, J. (1988) *Bridge to Calmer Waters – A study of a Bridge Families Scheme,* Barnardo's.

Wilson, J. (1991) *The Story of Tracy Beaker,* London: Corgi Yearling.